Flowers in the Desert

A Spirituality of the Bible

Demetrius Dumm, O.S.B.

Saint Vincent Archabbey Publications
300 Fraser Purchase Road
Latrobe, Pennsylvania 15650-2690
http://benedictine.stvincent.edu/

Scripture quotations are from The New English Bible,
© The Delegates of the Oxford University Press and
the Syndics of the Cambridge University Press 1961, 1970.
Reprinted by permission.

Library of Congress Cataloging-in-Publication Data

Dumm, Demetrius, 1923-
    Flowers in the desert: a spirituality of the Bible/
Demetrius Dumm
    p. cm.
    Originally published: New York: Paulist Press, c1987.
    Includes bibliographical references and indexes.
    ISBN 0-9708216-0-3
    1. Spiritual life - Biblical teaching. I. Title.

BS680.S7D86 2001
248-dc21   2001019178
                        CIP

Printed in the United States of America
Saint Vincent Archabbey Publications
300 Fraser Purchase Road
Latrobe, Pennsylvania 15650-2690

Cover photo and book design by Kimberley A. Opatka-Metzgar,
Saint Vincent Archabbey Publications

CONTENTS

Foreword   1

Part One — The Call

1   Exodus and Creation   5
2   Event-Centered Revelation   22
3   Our Response to God's Saving Event   35

Part Two — The Adventure

4   The Journey   57
5   Prophetic Guidance   77
6   Living in Hope   96
7   Traveling Together   109

Part Three — The Homecoming

8   Letting Go   135
9   The Resurrection as Homecoming   154
    Bibliography   169
    Indexes   171

To
Clare Ann

a special niece,
whose struggle to recover
from a serious accident
taught me so much about
faith, love, courage and
the David-spirit

Foreword

I have named my book **FLOWERS IN THE DESERT** because it is about the promise and pain of a human life that is truly open to God's wonderful mystery. This is a mystery that calls one to unselfish loving and therefore to a certain loss of understanding and control — it takes us into the desert. But it also gives life a new and profound meaning as it provides a sense of having found the way at last — it reveals surprising and exquisite desert flowers. Losing control and gaining wisdom thus represent another facet of the biblical paradox of life lost only to be found again.

My book is therefore about biblical spirituality. The word, spirituality, can be used in many ways. Here it is understood as a body of teachings about the meaning and purpose of human existence derived from a religious or transcendent revelation. As such, it is sharply distinguished from secular philosophy which limits its observations to this *saeculum*, to the here-and-now, and cannot therefore accept the validity of divine sources of revelation.

There can be as many different spiritualities as there are distinctive religious revelations. *Biblical* spirituality is, of course, derived from the sacred writings of the Bible. All Christian spiritualities are based to some extent on the Bible. However, this biblical influence can vary greatly and one of the purposes of this book is to argue for a more biblically-centered Christian spirituality. This has been a very congenial task for me because it is so completely in harmony with the authentic monastic tradition.

I am grateful to my Benedictine community for many years of support, and to my Benedictine confreres at Savannah, Georgia, for gracious hospitality as I labored there on my manuscript. I am grateful also to the Mary J. Donnelly Foundation of Pittsburgh, Pennsylvania, for a grant that partially defrayed the cost of my sabbatical leave. I owe special gratitude to my family for constant love, to many friends who have affirmed me and urged me to write this book and to my many former students whose generous response gave me added incentive to delve into the treasury of biblical wisdom. Special thanks go also to my confrere, Thomas Hart, who skillfully converted my scribbling into a beautiful computer printout.

Part One:

The Call

1
Exodus and Creation

The Exodus of Israel from the bondage of Egyptian oppression was the central event of the entire Old Testament. It was here that a dispirited and unorganized band of slaves met God and became a chosen people. Everything written in the Old Testament presupposed the Exodus, was written in the light of Exodus and would not have been written had there been no Exodus. Even the story of creation and the patriarchal sagas reflected the light of Exodus. This was in fact Israel's own creation story because it was here that she left the darkness and the empty and the void to find meaning and purpose in life. It was here that she first heard the creative call of the Lord.

BONDAGE

The event of Exodus is composed of three elements or moments: bondage, liberation and covenant. The moment of bondage encompasses much more than the simple fact of bondage as an historical situation. Israel's experience of oppression was real and painful and historical but it became a moment in the process of salvation only when it was personally acknowledged and accepted. Bondage alone leads to nothing; bondage acknowledged opens the way to salvation.

The Israelites had lived in slavery for a long time but nothing had happened: "Years passed, and the king of Egypt died, but the Israelites still groaned in slavery" (Exod 2:23). (Biblical quotations are from the *New English Bible*.) The situation changed completely, however, when they finally acknowledged their helplessness and cried out for assistance: "They cried out, and their appeal for rescue from their slavery rose up to God. He heard their groaning and remembered his covenant with Abraham, Isaac and Jacob; he saw the plight of Israel, and he took heed of it" (Exod 2:23-25). Commentators have noted that the biblical author does not say to whom the slaves cried out. It is very doubtful that they would have remembered the Patriarchs, those shadowy figures of four hundred years earlier. In fact, they cried out to anyone who might be good enough to take pity on them; it was God who "remembered" his own goodness and noted the promises prompted by that goodness and decided to have pity on them.

In a very real sense, all humans are born in "Egypt," in bondage. We are called to be free, but we are not born free. In the case of the Israelites, the bondage was clearly physical because they were restricted in their behavior and were forced to labor without recompense. It was also psychological: they were valued only for their productivity; they were unwanted, merely tolerated, dehumanized. Finally, their bondage was spiritual for they were left with no hope.

We are well acquainted with all these forms of bondage. Our bondage is more likely to be psychological and spiritual and its causes may be more subtle. We may not feel valued or appreciated; we may be paralyzed by fear or guilt or anxiety; we may be in the grip of some addiction; we may lack the liberating experience of a God who is not only powerful but also compassionate and caring. In some respects, being in this condition is no more than being human. There may be differences in degree but even those who have begun to move toward freedom remain partially in bondage. And, as in the case of Israel, the way out of oppression begins with an acknowledgement of need, a cry for help. It is this that triggers the divine "remembrance"; it is this cry that sets off alarms in heaven. The biblical story of Israel's initial bondage and of God's response to her plea for help is written to remind all generations of men and women that such a plea, made in the truth of acknowledged need, cannot be ignored by the real and caring God of Exodus.

LIBERATION

The essence of the Exodus event was God's mighty act of liberation. This could not have happened without acknowledged need and it led to covenant but the heart of the matter was liberation. This reminds us that salvation is never anything but liberation. To offer as salvation anything other than freedom is therefore to commit fraud. God took a terrible risk in giving freedom to Israel and those who preach the biblical message must be willing to take the same risk. Otherwise their preaching will produce even worse bondage as it simply increases guilt and gives no hope of forgiveness.

The first step in the carefully orchestrated process by which God gave Israel freedom was the call of Moses. It was necessary to find a fitting agent for this delicate task. God found Moses tending the flock and appeared to him out of the mysterious wilderness (Exod 3:1), catching his attention with a burning bush that was not consumed. The message was plain and clear:

> I have indeed seen the misery of my people in Egypt. I have heard their outcry against their slave-masters. I have taken heed of their sufferings, and have come down to rescue them from the power of Egypt, and to bring them up out of that country into a fine, broad land; it is a land flowing with milk and honey. . . (Exod 3:7-8).

God took pity on those slaves who were the heirs of Abraham, Isaac and Jacob; he decided that they must be released from their narrow, confined existence and be allowed to run like children at recess in that fine, broad land for which they were destined.

Moses did not have long to wonder why this was being announced to him. "Come now; I will send you to Pharaoh and you shall bring my people Israel out of Egypt" (Exod 3:10). Moses was stunned. Surely God must have known that he had killed a man in Egypt and was now a fugitive from justice. " 'But who am I,' Moses said to God, 'that I should go to Pharaoh, and that I should bring the Israelites out of Egypt' "(Exod 3:11)? Moses twisted and turned to evade the call. He asked God to identify himself, only to receive the mysterious name "I am" (Exod 3:14). He declared his inability to speak (and so to lead) but God provided Aaron (Exod 4:10-14).

This extended dialogue is meant to underline one crucial fact: the salvation that is to come will be God's work and not the work of Moses. Moses will play an important role but only God's action will be truly decisive. God might very well have said to Moses: "I fully agree that you cannot do it; I know that even better than you do. But you and I together can do it!" Moses was only the first in a long list of ministers of God's saving message who would be tempted to pull back from some apparently hopeless situation because of personal shortcomings. The human agent must make the effort before God will join the fray and bring the victory.

When Moses went to Egypt, he took with him the staff which represented God's power to bring about the plagues and finally break the stubborn resistance of Pharaoh. A cursory reading of these passages might suggest that God thus broke the power of Pharaoh by means of his own superior strength. Such an interpretation would really miss the point entirely. God's power is clearly superior to that of any tyrant but it was not this kind of power that brought freedom to the slaves. This kind of coercive power does not really produce freedom; it merely replaces one tyrant with another. God may choose to show this kind of power occasionally to get our attention or when nothing else can be understood but the power he cherishes and which alone liberated the slaves from Egypt is the gentle and irresistible power of *loving kindness*. This is God's *hesed*, his gracious mercy, the attribute of God that Israel liked most to remember. This is that mysterious goodness that caused God to be concerned about unattractive slaves, to love and cherish them, to choose and claim them. It was the experience of this goodness that liberated those dispirited and despairing slaves and gave them the courage and confidence to defy the power of Pharaoh and to walk out of their prison! Israel never ceased to wonder at this miracle.

Moses wielded his staff with impressive results but the real gift and genius of Moses was his ability to communicate to those slaves the love of God that he himself had experienced. He was an effective witness to them. The people saw the signs that Moses performed and were duly impressed but it was something more subtle that passed from Moses to them and that made all the difference. The Bible merely hints at it because it is not something that can readily be put into words: "They heard the Lord had shown his concern for the Israelites and seen their misery; and they bowed themselves to the ground in worship" (Exod 4:31). This "hearing" is the beginning of saving faith. What they heard was nothing less than the powerful word of creation that conquered chaos and fear and brought the light of meaning and purpose into their lives. To be loved in this way is to escape from the prison of low self-esteem, to find dignity and identity and inner confidence. To hear this loving, creating word is to begin to be saved.

In this context it is possible to appreciate the dramatic story of the ten plagues. No doubt there is a kernel of historical truth in them but they are essentially literarily embellished accounts to illustrate the miracle that lies at the heart of the Exodus event — the miracle of the enlivening of dead people through the experienced love of God. Thus, the spectacular elements in the story are simply the signs of a deeper and truly miraculous story of spiritual rebirth. It is for this reason that the Exodus story is such an appropriate liturgical reading for both Jewish Passover and Christian Easter.

Perhaps the most important lesson to be drawn from this crucial moment of the central event of the Old Testament is the truth that liberation or salvation comes from gentle love and not brutal power. The human way to make things happen is to amass power and to use it ruthlessly, whether it is for annexing another country or for insisting on one's own television program. The divine way is to love and to care and to nurture; it is to be considerate and thoughtful. From Moses to Jesus, the Bible urges us to give up the ultimately ineffective human way and to adopt the truly effective divine way.

COVENANT

The Exodus experience created a special bond between God and the Israelites. It was like the bond between a drowning man and his rescuer, for God had found them in a desperate situation and had given them new life and hope. When Israel recited the story of her origins she left no doubt about her desperation and God's part in her escape:

> My father was a homeless Aramaean who went down to Egypt . . . But the Egyptians ill-treated us, humiliated us and imposed cruel slavery upon us. Then we cried to the Lord the God of our fathers for help, and he listened to us . . . and so the Lord brought us out of Egypt with a strong hand and outstretched arm, with terrifying deeds, and with signs and portents. He brought us to this place and gave us this land, a land flowing with milk and honey (Deut 26:5-9).

The Hebrew word for "homeless" refers to sheep that have strayed from the flock and are as good as dead since the wolf is never far away. Hence, some translations render it "wandering" or "perishing." Israel in slavery was lost, had no meaning or purpose, was wandering aimlessly. God found her in that tragic situation and loved her, claiming her for himself and making her a chosen people. To have no sense of purpose or direction in life is to be close to death; to feel chosen and cherished is to find new life.

Thus, the covenant was far more than a contract between God and Israel. It was a profoundly personal relationship that involved an exchange of love and a pledging of loyalty. It was more like a marriage than a contract and, like a marriage, it was expected to grow and deepen as the partners came to know each other better in the vicissitudes of life. On God's part there was a pledge of unfailing presence with his people: "I will walk to and fro among you" (Lev 26:12). Israel would be expected to respond in love and gratitude in a way that would mark them as God's people: "I will become your God and you will become my people" (Lev 26:12). The remainder of the Old Testament is to a large extent the story of the ups and downs of that relationship, for Israel was to discover that God's presence could seem like absence and God would find in Israel both infidelity and childlike devotion.

In the beginning, however, there was only euphoria as Israel fondled this new thing called freedom. Psalm 114 tried to capture this moment:

> When Israel came out of Egypt, . . . the sea looked and ran away; Jordan turned back. The mountains skipped like rams, the hills like young sheep . . . Dance, 0 earth, at the presence of the Lord, at the presence of the God of Jacob, who turned the rock into a pool of water, the granite cliff into a fountain (vss. 1, 3-4, 7-8).

Rare joy indeed that caused staid and massive mountains to leap and skip like spring lambs! The words of God are no less poetic:

"You have seen with your own eyes what I did to Egypt, and how I have carried you on eagles' wings and brought you here to me" (Exod 19:4). The covenant was therefore, first and foremost, a celebration of the wonderful exchange of love between God and Israel. Only after that was there concern about the use of that freedom in a moral and responsible way.

For that reason, the heart of the covenant was the celebrated "Shema^c" of Israel:

> Hear (shema^c), 0 Israel, the Lord is our God, one Lord, and you must love the Lord your God with all your heart and

> soul and strength. These commandments which I give you this day are to be kept in your heart; you shall repeat them to your children, and speak of them indoors and out of doors, when you lie down and when you rise. Bind them as a sign on the hand and wear them as a phylactery on the forehead; write them up on the door-posts of your houses and on your gates (Deut 6:4-9).

The Lord is to be loved exclusively because it was he alone who brought the Israelites out of the land of bondage. This love was to be so personal and so real that it would amount to a constant distraction as Israel went about her duties in history. The awareness of God's presence and goodness should never be totally absent even at her most preoccupied moments. Moreover, that awareness would be actualized and nurtured in fully conscious times of deliberate prayer and adoration.

COVENANT RESPONSIBILITY

The Ten Commandments (Decalogue) were a first and fundamental attempt to spell out some of the implications of Israel's love and gratitude in the realm of daily living. They are found in both Exodus (20:2-17) and Deuteronomy (5:6-21) but the older version is that of Exodus.

An indispensable and perhaps the most important element of the Decalogue is its preamble: "I am the Lord your God who brought you out of Egypt, out of the land of slavery" (Exod 20:2). It is indispensable and critically important because it specifies the only proper motivation for observing the precepts which follow. The Ten Commandments are not simply standards of conduct to be kept for whatever reason. They are guidelines for a freedom that is presupposed and which derives from the experienced love and goodness of God. The preamble says, in effect, that if one has not yet been delivered from the "land of slavery," he should not read any further but should search instead for the love that alone can provide that freedom. If this warning is disregarded, the commandments will become occasions for false pride when kept or crippling guilt when disobeyed. In either case, they will not have served the purpose for which they were intended. These commandments are not to be observed therefore because God is stronger than we are but because God has loved us and wants us to use our freedom properly. This serves as a solemn reminder that, in matters of religion, loving and freeing people must always precede commanding and holding them responsible.

The first commandment reads: "You shall have no other god to set against me" (Exod 20:3). The first obligation of the newly liberated Israelites was one of exclusive loyalty to the Lord. This is based upon the fact that it was the Lord alone who delivered them from slavery. They may be tempted to turn to other more indulgent gods but that path is blocked by the simple truth that those gods were not present when Israel was rescued from death and cannot therefore rightly claim any recognition (even if they existed). The other gods may promise much but they have done nothing! Note again how much the experience of liberation is presupposed.

The second commandment forbids idolatry: "You shall not make a carved image for yourself nor the likeness of anything. . . You shall not bow down to them or worship them; for I, the Lord your God, am a jealous God" (Exod 20:4-5). To understand properly the intent of this commandment, one must be aware of a popular religious assumption of those ancient times, namely, that the physical, crafted image of a deity could be used in a magical way to control and manipulate the god so represented. God here forbids the Israelites to acknowledge the existence of rival gods, but the commandment was also understood by Israel to forbid the crafting of any images of the Lord. Such images would not only endanger the mystery of God but they would also, when used superstitiously, violate the personal relationship between him and his people. To attempt to manipulate the Lord would be offensive and insulting because it would imply that he, who had delivered them, was unable or unwilling to listen to their plea. This is wrong because it shows a lack of trust, and a liberated people should be expected to trust their savior.

The third commandment reads: "You shall not make wrong use of the name of the Lord your God: the Lord will not leave unpunished the man who misuses his name" (Exod 20:7). (The traditional Catholic numbering incorrectly combines the second and third commandments.) This commandment is similar to the second in the sense that it forbids magic. Here it is a question, not of voodoo dolls or such, but of the divine name used as part of a magical incantation. Once again, such a practice is forbidden because it treats God, not as a loving, caring savior, but as an impersonal, impassive deity. This is wrong for Israel because they have experienced God's love and should therefore trust his goodness.

The fourth commandment concerns the Sabbath: "Remember to keep the sabbath day holy. You have six days to labor and do all your work. But the seventh day is a sabbath of the Lord your God; . . . for in six days the Lord made heaven and earth, the sea, and all that is in them, and on the seventh day he rested. Therefore the Lord blessed the sabbath day and declared it holy" (Exod 20:8-11). The Sabbath commandment occupies a unique position in the Decalogue; it follows the commandments which are concerned with the Israelites' relationship with God and it precedes those which govern the relationship of Israelites with each other. It is therefore a transitional commandment which is still aware of the mystery of God but now focuses on that mystery as it is shared with all of creation.

It seems easy to affirm the mystery of God, for God appears to be distant and powerful. But that same divine mystery is present to some degree in every being that has come forth from the creative love of God. Every creature deserves therefore to be respected because of its share of divine mystery. One of the most powerful tendencies of man is to eliminate mystery in his life because it cannot be controlled and thus seems threatening to him. The most natural way for man to control the mystery in creation is through his labor. The Sabbath commandment orders the

Israelite to interrupt his labor every seventh day as a reminder that that labor is intended by God to release the mystery in life and not to crush it.

God had said in Genesis that man should "fill the earth and subdue it" (Gen 1:28) but in doing so he is to follow the example of God who did in fact subdue the chaos and darkness to create order and light but who did not thereby destroy the hidden beauty and goodness in creation. On the contrary, his creative labor called forth that beauty so that he needed to pause occasionally to admire what he had done and finally proclaimed that his creation was "very good" (Gen 1:31). Then God "ceased from all his work. God blessed the seventh day and made it holy, because on that day he ceased from all the work he had set himself to do" (Gen 2:2-3). God rested on the seventh day, not like a successful hunter standing over a trophy specimen, but like a good teacher who has dispelled the chaos of ignorance and released the creativity of his or her students. God's perfect observance of Sabbath in the creation story shows that labor is for increasing and enhancing the mystery and beauty that are obscured by chaos. Labor is not an end in itself; rather, it is to prepare for the enjoyment of released beauty and goodness.

Sabbath observance then will be characterized by a joyful and carefree spirit because one is finally able to "waste" time with God and with people as one contemplates and appreciates the beauty hidden in them. Herbert Richardson recalls how the Puritans of colonial New England placed special emphasis on the Sabbath and raised again the question about the possibility of Incarnation even if there had been no sin. Jesus then would have come simply to be with us, to be Emmanuel, to keep Sabbath with us! He uses a story to make his point:

> Suppose you visit a friend and discover on your arrival at his house that he is moving a heavy trunk. After you have helped him move it, he says, 'Thanks for coming over to help me move the trunk.' But you had not gone to visit him for this reason even though you were happy

to help him with the trunk when you discovered his need
(*Toward an American Theology*, p. 128).

In this scenario, Jesus is thanked for his labor of redemption and then dismissed. But the labor of redemption is complete only when it brings Sabbath presence and enjoyment, only when there is time for personal exchange and enjoyment after the trunk has been moved!

Human labor can also be redemptive since it strives to eliminate what is chaotic and meaningless in life but it must be careful not to destroy mystery in the process. It must be respectful; it must not be poisoned by ambition or greed or violence. Otherwise it will not lead to Sabbath, either on the seventh day or on the final day. For the final Sabbath is heaven and heaven is for people who have learned in this life to be more and more filled with wonder and ready for happy surprise.

The Sabbath spirit thus contradicts absolutely the spirit of Pharaonic power which values only control for the powerful elite and productivity from the powerless victims. Israel must make that ideal her own; she must labor resolutely to realize the potential of creation but she must know that happiness comes from gift, not labor; labor merely prepares for gift, for Sabbath.

The fifth commandment and those that follow it are concerned with critical areas of human life where mystery is most precious and most vulnerable. Thus the fifth commandment reads: "Honor your father and your mother, that you may live long in the land which the Lord your God is giving you" (Exod 20:12). It is not a question here of the obedience that children owe their parents. Even pagans knew that children must be obedient. There was no need of a special commandment to ensure what is evident to any reasonable person. What is commanded here is honor, respect and care for aged parents on the part of their grown-up children. In a society that is governed by merely human wisdom, old people will be considered useless and a burden. But in a community imbued with the divine wisdom expressed in Exodus, the special mystery and beauty of the aged will be revered and protected. Wherever worth is determined, not by productivity but by personal mystery and love, the aged will always be welcomed and cherished.

The sixth commandment forbids what is the primary threat to mystery, namely, violence: "You shall not commit murder" (Exod 20:13). Though only murder is expressly forbidden, the commandment involves far more than that brutal act. The whole spectrum of violence, psychic as well as physical, is included in this prohibition. All such violence diminishes life which is protected by God who alone can give it and has the right to take it. And where life is most defenseless and vulnerable it must be most carefully protected. The author does not have abortion in mind but the principle established here makes abortion one of the worst forms of violence against life, for fetal life is as precious as it is vulnerable.

The seventh commandment reads: "You shall not commit adultery" (Exod 20:14). Once again, although only marital infidelity is explicitly forbidden, the commandment embraces any attack on the delicate and very vulnerable relationship of love. Love is perhaps the most precious and mysterious of all human experiences. It defies explanation or analysis. One can read volumes about love and not know as much as is learned from five minutes of actual loving! But it is very vulnerable too and can easily be damaged or destroyed by seduction, envy or distrust. This commandment forbids such destructive behavior and thus strives to protect the precious mystery that made the Exodus possible.

The eighth commandment forbids another form of violence: "You shall not steal" (Exod 20:15). In the clan society of the Old Testament period, stealing was considered particularly odious because it not only deprived a person of the peaceful enjoyment of his goods but it also destroyed the trust which made it possible to live as a free community. Stealing is a sin against the very life of the community because of the chilling effect it has on the freedom and peace of everyone. When one person's goods are stolen, one hears locks closing in all the other homes and the whole community is a little less free than it was before and has a right to be. The precious, mysterious, vulnerable gift that is protected by this commandment is trust. This is the fresh air of the community; without it the community stifles.

The ninth commandment reads: "You shall not give false evidence against your neighbor" (Exod 20:16). If the Bible is preoccupied with any one sin, it is that of the deceitful and malicious tongue. Time and again, particularly in the Wisdom Literature, the destructiveness of the deceitful tongue is bemoaned. The precious, vulnerable reality that is safeguarded by this commandment is one's good name, one's reputation. It is almost impossible to protect oneself completely against attacks on one's honesty, integrity or motivation. Some mud always sticks! Here again, it is the trusting atmosphere of the community that is diminished or destroyed.

The tenth commandment warns against the corrosive effects of envy: "You shall not covet your neighbor's house; you shall not covet your neighbor's wife, his slave, his slave-girl, his ox, his ass, or anything that belongs to him" (Exod 20:17). (In a patriarchal society, where everything is viewed from the masculine perspective, a man's wife is listed among his blessings, the riches of his household. The commandment could just as well read: You shall not covet your neighbor's husband.) What is prohibited by this commandment is the subtle but very real blighting effect that is produced by an envious and resentful attitude. Almost everyone can recall the unpleasant experience of a visitor whose eyes roam over one's possessions appraisingly and who then proceeds to bewail the fact that he does not have this or that article. One's spontaneous reaction is to say: "Why don't you take it since you have already partially destroyed my enjoyment of it!" Such covetousness diminishes the enjoyment of one's blessings and in Israel where there were few wealthy people every person had the right to such peaceful enjoyment of his modest household. (Needless to say, in an unjust society where goods are hoarded by the few, the situation is altogether different and "covetousness" becomes a yearning for justice!)

Thus, the Ten Commandments are ten ways of channeling

freedom and strength so that they lead to deep respect for mystery and goodness in every aspect of life and to gentle, loving concern for every creature and for all the delicate, beautiful relationships that bind those creatures together. The Ten Commandments are not ten flaming hoops that we must clear in order to gain heaven! They are ten examples of how to use freedom responsibly and when they are observed there will be other challenges because freedom to love is an opportunity that lasts forever.

CREATION

Every society that is concerned about the present purpose and direction of its world must ask questions about the origin of that world. The Israelites were no exception. In fact, they had two creation stories: the first (Gen 1:1-2:4) tells how a world was prepared for man who appears as the climax of God's creative activity; the second (Gen 2:5-25) begins with the creation of man and then provides other creatures in response to his needs. The two stories are essentially complementary.

The biblical author could not have received this information by tradition since millions of years are involved. Nor can it be assumed that God gave him special revelation. A careful study of these accounts clearly indicates that the author merely combined his conviction about the goodness of God as it was experienced in the Exodus with the popular creation stories current at his time. The result is a "corrected" version of those popular stories but corrected only in regard to the role of the creator god for this is the only part of the story with religious implications and that is the sole interest of the author. Unlike Marduk, the Babylonian creator, who struggled violently to make the world, the Hebrew God is serenely sovereign and brings the world into being with a simple command. Since the true God shares no power with an evil deity, he alone is responsible for creation. Since he was discovered by Israel in the Exodus experience of liberation through love, his new world must be good, beautiful and unspoiled. Creation coming from the hand of God was as beautiful as a drop of rain on a spring leaf!

This lovely world replaced a nothingness that was described as *tohu wa bohu,* empty and void. It was a condition of chaos and darkness, without meaning or purpose. What the author was really describing here was the experience of Israel in the oppression and slavery of Egypt. He then projects the experience of Israel onto the universal screen, reasoning with some logic that the condition of the whole universe must have been similar to that of the slaves in Egypt before God spoke his creative word of love among them. In effect, God "liberated" the universe from nothingness in the same way that he liberated the Israelites from their experience of nothingness in the slavery of Egypt. It is for this reason that the first effect of God's creative activity was light, which symbolizes meaning, just as the first experience of Israel was the discovery of meaning and purpose in her life. The emphasis on distinguishing and ordering on the subsequent days of creation is meant to contrast with the chaos and confusion and aimlessness of a life of oppression. Moreover, since Israel sensed that God cherished his gentle loving more than his coercive power, he is pictured admiring his creation's goodness rather than its massive greatness.

The Israelites were very conscious of the fact that, though their God had conquered chaos, he had not destroyed it. Accordingly, the work of creation goes on as each generation finds itself once again the arena of the struggle between slavery and freedom, darkness and light, chaos and order. This is the context within which one must view the stories in the gospels about Jesus expelling demons. In the Bible, demons are agents of chaos; they represent the continuing power of the original darkness. Jesus came to initiate a new creation and must therefore confront the representatives of chaos who immediately recognize him as their natural enemy.

When the biblical author considered human creation, he was satisfied to note simply that we humans belong to two worlds — to the physical world through our bodies and to the spiritual world through our spirits. We belong to the physical world but our spirits put us in touch with God. At the heart of this spiritual gift was the ability to choose, which made humans in some sense like God. This special ability allowed them to reach toward their Creator but also to reject their status as creatures and to taste the bitter fruit of sin and shame. It also permitted them to repent, however, and when that happened the goodness of God that created them became the goodness that forgave and restored.

These profound truths are expressed in a deceptively simple manner but they remain the foundation stones of biblical religion. Thus, the themes of chaos, sin, bondage, love and liberation continue to recur until Jesus inaugurates the final age and gives the definitive meaning to love and liberation in his Passion, Death and Resurrection. The whole process is dominated by the love of God — a love that calls being out of nothingness, slaves out of Egypt and sinners to salvation.

2

Event-Centered Revelation

THE GOD WHO ACTS

God revealed himself to the Israelites by acting in their history. He did not just speak consoling words or offer advice or teach eternal truths. He did that too but, first and foremost, he entered their terrible situation of bondage, shared their pain and frustration and then severed those bonds and led them to freedom. "I broke the bars of your yoke and enabled you to walk upright" (Lev 26:13). This means that biblical revelation is centered in a saving event. It is not a religious philosophy though it is full of religious truths; it is not a book of ethics though it speaks often about moral behavior; it is a history, a record of events, a narrative of salvation. It is not however a history in the sense of a mere record of the past; it is interpreted history which is as much concerned with the meaning of events as it is with their reality. Thus, the biblical author certainly wishes to affirm that there was an historical exodus from Egypt, but the way in which he tells the story is concerned more with the meaning of the event than with exact historical description.

The great Jewish philosopher, Martin Buber, states the matter admirably:

> The Bible presents us with a story only, but this story is theology; biblical theology is narrated theology. The Bible cannot be really comprehended if it is not comprehended

in this way: as a doctrine that is nothing but history, and as a history that is nothing but doctrine. The history of the world comes to us as the history of Israel; and in this, and only in this and not outside of it, do we receive the teaching as to the purpose of the world and the purpose of Israel, both in one (*On The Bible,* p. 26).

Buber thus bears witness to the fact that the biblical authors were the first to take history seriously. For them, religious meaning is not something imposed on history from above but it is revealed and expressed in and through history. Buber was speaking of the Hebrew scriptures but what he says is even more obvious in the New Testament. The revelation of God in Jesus is seen most clearly, not in his spoken words, but in his actions, and essentially in the actions of the climactic Paschal event of Passion, Death and Resurrection. Jesus "spoke" most eloquently when he was virtually silent as he acted out the new and definitive Exodus event of passage from death to life.

If biblical revelation is centered in saving event, it follows that the proper mode for the expression of this revelation is narrative. Another well-known theologian, Emil Brunner, has noted that the relationship of God and man in the Bible "is not a timeless or static relation from the world of ideas, and only for such is doctrine an adequate form: rather the relation is an event, and hence narration is the proper form to describe it. The decisive word-form in the language of the Bible is not the substantive, as in Greek, but the verb, the word of action" (*The Divine-Human Encounter,* p. 47). When Brunner points to the contrast between Greek and Hebrew thought and expression he reminds us that we are heirs of Greek civilization which shaped our Western culture. We, like the Greeks, tend to see the substantive first and to yearn for definition, whereas the men of the Bible gave priority to the verb and were primarily concerned about direction or destiny. Martin Buber captures the contrast well:

Of all the Orientals the Jew is the most obvious antithesis of the Greek. The Greek wants to master the world, the

Jew, to perfect it. For the Greek the world exists; for the Jew, it becomes. The Greek confronts it; the Jew is involved with it. The Greek apprehends it under the aspect of measure, the Jew as intent. For the Greek the deed is in the world, for the Jew the world is in the deed (*On Judaism*, p. 66).

We must therefore make a conscious effort to enter this somewhat alien environment where "the world is in the deed," where story carries more religious truth than mere doctrine and where a creed begins, "My father was a homeless Aramaean . . ." (Deut 26:5), rather than, "I believe in one God."

This primacy of event as a bearer of revelation distinguishes the Judaeo-Christian tradition from all the other major religions. Buddhism and Confucianism, for example, are centered in the teaching of a great religious philosopher. "Confucius say . . ." is the formula for revelation. In Israel, however, the teaching of Moses simply draws the implications out of the Exodus event. And in Christianity the contrast is even sharper for, though Jesus was a great teacher and his words are full of profound truth, it was his dying in virtual silence and his resurrection to glory that constituted the fountainhead of Christian revelation. The message of Jesus about the meaning and purpose of human existence is centered in that crucial event and in its implications for the true meaning of human success and happiness. Like Confucius, Jesus said many true and important things but the real message of Jesus is in what he did! It is only slightly simplistic to say: Confucius say; Jesus do!

This centrality of story as the biblical bearer of religious truth is illustrated by one of those delightful stories attributed to the great Jewish mystic of Eastern Europe, Baal Shem Tov:

The ancient *tsaddik* went to an exact spot in the forest, told the story, lit a fire, and offered prayer, and the miracle happened. In the next generation, the rabbi forgot the spot, but he told the story, lit the fire, and prayed, and the miracle happened. Years passed, and the next rabbi forgot the spot and never lit the fire, but he told the story and prayed, and the miracle happened.

> Generations later, the rabbi forgot the spot, didn't light
> the fire and couldn't remember the prayer, but he told
> the story — and still the miracle happened.

For Christianity, as for Israel, "telling the story" will always be the one indispensable element in continuing the miracle of Exodus and Resurrection. Small wonder then that the high point of the Eucharist, by which the central Christian event is re-enacted liturgically, is a narrative of what Jesus did the night before he died.

We must constantly remind ourselves of the story-mode of biblical revelation because of the eminently practical implications it has for the manner in which we receive that revelation. For if the saving revelation is given primarily in event and story, we can truly receive that revelation only by entering into and in some way sharing the experience of that event. It is not enough to hear about it; we must go beyond the words to the event itself; we must be able to say that we too have begun to participate in what happened there. In the Jewish Seder (Passover) service to this day we hear the words: "In every generation each one ought to regard himself as though he had personally come out of Egypt." And the Christian Eucharist is a drama of action which requires active participation and is concluded with communion between the Actor and the believer.

The possibility of keeping a great saving event alive and present so that all generations will have an opportunity to share in it is based on the fact of God's original participation in that event. Since God is not confined to time and space, his participation in the event gives it an eternal and timeless side which can be related to any subsequent historical moment. Liturgical or ritual re-enactment becomes the vehicle then for this mysterious but very actual saving moment. However, though this moment is mysterious, it is not magical, for the human participants must bring to it sincere faith and a readiness to be converted in accordance with the meaning of the saving event that is liturgically reproduced. The readings from Scripture and the comments of the leader are designed to stir up that faith and to dispose those present for more fruitful participation.

From this perspective, one can see how important it is to discover a truly reliable access to these saving events. The ancient and traditional Catholic practice of liturgical re-enactment joined to appropriate biblical texts and accurate commentary remains the classic and most effective method. It is true that the biblical text itself is an avenue to the events described in the Bible but reading the Bible is no cure-all. The hundreds of thousands of biblical words were written originally in a foreign language and reflect a culture very different from our own. They need to be interpreted by careful scholarship. At the same time, even the best scholarly opinion is not an adequate basis for religious commitment. The believing community, under wise and experienced leadership and fully cognizant of the work of scholars, is the best medium for presenting those saving events to each successive generation. One who is a scholar only may discourse eloquently about the meaning of the Bible but lack the sincerity and simplicity required for entering into the saving events described there. Just as truly, a simplistic faith that rejects the aid of scholarship will also be lacking in the humility and truthfulness which alone open the way to those gracious events.

BIBLICAL EVENT AS CREATIVE AFFIRMATION

It is impossible to go back in time to the original saving event. However, since the love of God that made that event possible is as constant and available now as it ever was, it is possible to discover that love and to experience the creative affirmation that is its first effect at any moment in time. It is true that even at the beginning one may sense the eventual cost of yielding to this love but the primary experience is one of delightful euphoria at being chosen, affirmed and therefore given value, respect, confidence and freedom. This will usually be only the beginning of a movement toward salvation because the bonds of guilt and low self-esteem are not so easily severed. But it is a critical and blessed moment because the course of one's life has been changed, the ice of winter is breaking and yielding as the newly discovered sun calls forth a springtime of life and beauty. In nature, this is always a dramatic event for one can hardly believe in February that this scene of ice and snow and frozen ground will soon be lush and vibrant with spring growth. God's love, usually mediated through human love and concern, works a similar miracle when a defeated and dejected person suddenly finds new hope and is inwardly renewed. When one begins to participate in the saving event through the wonder of the experience of love, one begins to understand the meaning of God's call to new life. This is truly a moment of creation, of awakening to new meaning and purpose.

THE BAPTISM OF JESUS

As the evangelists reviewed the career that brought Jesus to the supreme moment of Death and Resurrection, they realized that it all began with a momentous discovery which they attempt to capture in the story of the Baptism of Jesus. The earliest and simplest account is found in Mark 1:9-11:

> It happened at this time that Jesus came from Nazareth in Galilee and was baptized in the Jordan by John. At the moment when he came up out of the water, he saw the heavens torn open and the Spirit, like a dove, descending upon him. And a voice spoke from heaven: 'Thou art my Son, my Beloved; on thee my favor rests.'

It would be difficult to state the matter more succinctly than Mark has done. Actually, the baptism is not described at all. Much more attention is given to the consequences, climaxing in a powerful affirmation of Jesus by God, who identifies himself as Father.

In Matthew's more detailed version (3:13-17), a question is

raised about the appropriateness of a baptism for Jesus: "John tried to dissuade him. 'Do you come to me?' he said; 'I need rather to be baptized by you' " (3:14). Jesus insisted, however, and John overcame his scruples. John's reluctance can be understood if one sees baptism only as a rite of repentance and therefore unnecessary for the innocent. However, that was only one aspect of the Jewish baptismal practice. It was indeed an act that expressed regret and repentance for sin but, on the positive side, it was a plea for the coming of the Lord. Sins were renounced because they were seen as obstacles to that coming. When Jesus insisted on being baptized, he was not renouncing sinfulness but was taking his place with all those in Israel who were saying: "We are ready, Lord; please make this the moment of your Messianic salvation."

That this was in fact the context of Mark's baptismal story is confirmed by his reference to the heavens being torn open (1:10) which is an image borrowed from Isaiah: "Why didst thou not rend the heavens and come down?" (64:1). This occurs in a section that describes at length Israel's yearning for a new Exodus and a new creation. The baptism was not therefore merely an episode in the private life of Jesus. Jesus joined an Israel that was crying out in anguish for the promised Messianic visitation that would usher in the new age of victory and peace; Jesus joins all of us who still look for final salvation.

It is precisely from this perspective that Mark describes, in symbolic language, the consequences of the baptism of Jesus. First of all, the heavens are torn open, certainly from God's side, to signify that, since Jesus is now standing with Israel, God is ready too. The presence of Jesus triggers the long awaited saving action of God. This rending of the heavens permits the Spirit to appear in the likeness of a dove. This is the Spirit who hovered, bird-like, over the primeval deep (Gen 1:2) and who is always associated in the Bible with moments of creation. This appearance of the dove-like Spirit signifies, therefore, the dawning of a new era, a new world, another creation.

This new creation does not directly affect the physical world.

It is rather a new age of spiritual awareness and opportunity that is announced, and the nature of this new creation is revealed in the words spoken to Jesus from heaven: "Thou art my Son, my Beloved; on thee my favor rests" (Mark 1:11). The first part of this powerful statement is borrowed from Psalm 2:7: "You are my son; this day I become your father." These words are to be fulfilled in the future Messiah. The second part is from Isaiah 42:1: "Here is my servant, whom I uphold, my chosen one in whom I delight." This is the mysterious Suffering Servant who will atone for the sins of his people. But these words take on dramatic fresh meaning in this new context. The new creation is centered in a powerful influx of creative love which reveals God as Father, as loving parent, in a way that had never been imagined before. God's love is now available to create free and loving sons and daughters, to give the kind of confidence that was given to Jesus in this first moment of his public ministry. Of course, our relationship to God cannot be exactly like that of his only-begotten Son but it is closer to it than most of us dare believe.

Every Christian baptism contains a renunciation of sinfulness but it is, most of all, an affirmation by God. If one is baptized as an infant, the experience of baptism will need to be captured later, not only in adult regret for sin, but much more so in the experience of a loving, caring family and community through whom the creative love of God is expressed. Where this does not happen, baptism remains a seed that has not sprouted and grown and borne fruit. Every Christian life must begin therefore with an experience of affirmation which alone will make it possible to know God as Father and which will produce that identity and confidence and freedom that will permit the following of Jesus in love and service. Hearing the Good News is not just hearing the Gospel read or preached; it is experiencing love for one's own sake, for one's freedom. A gospel that is used for threatening people or to support authoritarian control is really the Bad News! Moreover, it is a betrayal of the true gospel that preaches love first and, only after that is assured, speaks about responsibility.

THE WORD THAT BECAME FLESH

The Gospel of John offers a very different perspective from that of the Synoptic gospels. For John, the career of Jesus begins, not at baptism as in Mark, nor with the birth in Bethlehem as in Matthew and Luke, but in the farthest reaches of eternity, before the dawn of creation. "When all things began, the Word already was" (John 1:1). This Word is, in some mysterious manner both one with God and distinct from God. It is one with God and therefore knows the secrets of God; it is distinct from God and becomes the vehicle of God's self-revelation. It is for this reason that it is called the Word of God; in the Word God speaks himself! God's self-revelation is already a sign of his essential goodness for he is first known as one who reaches out to others.

The first manifestation of this divine exuberance was the creation of the universe: ". . . through him all things came to be; no single thing was created without him" (John 1:3). This original word expressed in creation spoke clearly of God's love and goodness: "All that came to be was alive with his life, and that life was the light of men" (John 1:4). The original creation was fresh and beautiful, alive with God's own vitality. It was full of blessing for us too for the universe was made to be our garden; it had all the qualities of that blessed light of the first day (Gen 1:3): warmth, security, confidence, joy. It was a beautiful garden smiling back at its divine sun. Sin brought some shadows into that garden but it could never completely distort creation's beauty: "The light shines on in the dark, and the darkness has never mastered it" (John 1:5).

A new creative impulse of the Word occurred in Exodus when the goodness of God was manifested in the free choice of Israel and in the revelation of Torah. This Torah-word became richer, more mysterious in the mouths of the prophets and took on new colors with the Wisdom writers. But it was always beneficent and creative. Finally, in the fullness of time, the Word appeared in the person of Jesus who recapitulated and perfected all previous revelations. He was the "last word" of God. However, though he spoke the truth and healed the sick, he was really accepted by only a few.

> He was in the world; but the world, though it owed its being to him, did not recognize him. He entered his own realm, and his own would not receive him. But to all who did receive him, to those who have yielded him their allegiance, he gave the right to become children of God . . . (John 1:10-12).

Raymond Brown (*The Gospel According to John,* Vol I, p.29), argues convincingly that this passage refers to Jesus because, for John, becoming children of God is a possibility that would exist only after the coming of Jesus (See John 3:3-8). Later on in the gospel, John shows clearly why so many failed to accept Jesus and his message: it was a message of love that not only gave freedom but also demanded the service of love. "Here lies the test: the light has come into the world, but men preferred darkness to light because their deeds were evil" (John 3:19). They preferred darkness because this permitted them to cling to their selfish and controlling ways.

If the Incarnation is announced already in verse 10, the emphasis in verse 14 shifts from the fact of Incarnation to its purpose: "So the Word became flesh; he came to dwell among us, and we saw his glory, such glory as befits the Father's only Son, full of grace and truth" (John 1:14). The divine Word took on a human nature so that the Father's love could be shared more fully with us, his beloved children. This love is intended to make it possible for us to live together in harmony and mutual support; it is intended to create vibrant and joyful human community, from the smallest family to the wide world of nations. God's final Word is, therefore, a word of love and God's purpose for creation is fulfilled when all that wonderful variety is filled with his love and lives in harmony.

John testifies that he and the other disciples "saw his glory,""that is, they recognized the presence of God in the human person of Jesus. "Glory" in the Bible refers to any sense-perceptible manifestation of God's presence in our world — from the luminous cloud of the Sinai journey to the luminous love that shone through Jesus and touched his disciples. This glory was such as one would expect to see in the only-begotten, uniquely-beloved Son of God. The love of God transfigured the human nature of Jesus so that he glowed with inner confidence and freedom. In Jesus, the disciples saw what the love of God can do in a human being who receives it fully. Jesus thus becomes the final and perfect manifestation of "grace and truth" which were the attributes of God most cherished by Israel. "Grace" translates *hesed* which means merciful, gracious love and expresses Israel's first and deepest experience of God, for this was that wonderful impulse that caused God to choose them as his own people. "Truth" translates *'emeth* which refers to the faithfulness and constancy of God in his loving of Israel. It was wonderful that God should have loved them; it was equally wonderful that he should not be fickle like humans but ever-faithful in his love for them. Jesus, in his loving unto death, is the perfect and enduring sign and guarantee of the Father's continued love and fidelity to all his children.

This revelation of the nature of God as One-who-loves is not presented as a statement of fact; it is expressed in history, in events. For nothing is more real and tangible than creation itself and this word is spoken to all in every moment of time. Israel enjoyed the special word of Torah spoken in her own historical idiom. Now Jesus is the Word spoken to all the world — a Word spoken to the heart more than to the mind. Those who dare to admit their hunger and who open their hearts to this Word will find their most personal history radically changed. Birth and death seem unreal in comparison to that event!

THE DISCOVERY OF GIFT IN LIFE

A word that captures in a special way the spirit of the Bible is the word "promise." Both Israelites and Christians are people of the promise. God truly entered human history and chose Israel in the event of Exodus just as Jesus truly became incarnate in our history "under Pontius Pilate." But these are only beginnings; we still await the fulfillment; we live in promise.

When Paul writes, in his letter to the Romans, that the justice of God has been at long last revealed in Jesus, he is not speaking of the justice that at the end will reward the good and punish the wicked. He is referring rather to the saving justice of God by which God is faithful to his promise of salvation, and therefore faithful to himself. This justice comes from the essential goodness of God and is not conditional in any way: "But now, quite independently of law, God's justice has been brought to light. The Law and the prophets both bear witness to it: it is God's way of righting wrong, effective through faith in Christ for all who have such faith — all, without distinction" (Rom 3:21-22). In Jesus, God's saving power is available to all; the only condition is in the recipient and concerns his faith.

Obviously, it is of great importance to understand what Paul means by faith. It is, of course, a gift of God but it also implies a free decision on our part. No one is forced to believe. Faith is too personal and mysterious to be defined but it can be described. Paul gives us a broad hint when he writes: ". . . all are justified by God's free grace alone . . ." (Rom 3:24). A literal translation reads: "they are justified after the manner of a gift by his favor." This is a redundant statement for the purpose of emphasizing the gift-quality of the faith-event. It is a free gift on the part of God; on the part of the believer it is the recognition and acceptance of gift. Paul insists on this gift-quality of faith: "The promise was made on the ground of faith, in order that it might be a matter of sheer grace . . ." (Rom 4:16).

Faith certainly involves an intellectual assent to the truths of revelation, as we have all been taught. But it also includes a profound, intuitional recognition of the gift-nature of all reality and, beyond that, the goodness and trustworthiness of God. There is enough evil and darkness in life to tempt one to question whether life is basically good. Faith is an awakening to the radical goodness in life, in spite of the very real evil that is also found there. Faith makes us ready for goodness, causes us to look for it in hidden and ambiguous places and enables us to call mystery what is often seen only as evil or defeat or disaster. Saint Thérèse of Lisieux expressed this faith-sensitivity most aptly when, though she was young and dying of consumption, she exclaimed, "Everything is a gift!" (*Sainte Thérèse: Derniers Entretiens,* p. 221). It was this kind of faith too that the author of Hebrews described as he surveyed the lives of the great men and women of the Bible and noted how they maintained their courage and trust in spite of adversity (Heb 11:1-40).

Paul goes on to say that this free gift of God that is recognized by faith is expressed most perfectly "through His (God's) act of liberation in the person of Christ" (Rom 3:24). Jesus is the one in whom henceforth we see the most perfect expression of God's love and goodness toward us and also the most perfect example of the response to that goodness in unquestioning faith and trust. No one was loved by God more than Jesus; no one responded more generously to that love than did Jesus. Every movement toward faith begins with God's love, experienced in real life, for faith can be found only in those who have first experienced the partial gift and are thus made free enough to risk, as Saint Thérèse did, that "Everything is a gift." Thus, revelation is not just an abstract truth; it is first and foremost an event, a divine act of love, and only through the experience of that event in one's own history is the birth of faith possible. We hear God's call when we experience his love as we enter into the event by which God has gifted all creation.

3

Our Response to God's Saving Event

Our response by faith to the love of God truly experienced in our lives is not something that is easily assumed or readily measured. Children commonly believe with the faith of their parents or some other trusted adult. There is frequently a crisis when the child is thrust out of that faith-womb. This often occurs when a young person goes away to college and it is sometimes mistaken for a loss of faith. Actually, it is usually only the loss of that parenting faith which must in any case be eventually replaced by one's own faith decision. It is fortunate if this crisis occurs in one's formative years and is accompanied by good advice. Otherwise, decision can be postponed almost indefinitely and that means a safe but puerile and unfruitful kind of faith.

More common and more dangerous than the undeveloped faith is a faith that is superficial. Many happily affirm the articles of a creed and accept the teachings of a church but still live very much like good pagans. They are not wicked people but neither are they really converted. The chief characteristic of this state is a sense of control. One believes in God and is careful to attend church and to pray but he is still in charge of his own life and what he does makes good sense. I used to think that the youthful Saint Paul was more fortunate than I because, not being a Christian, he was able to be converted. Now it is clear to me that I too must be converted from a relatively smug and secure faith, such as Paul enjoyed when he set out confidently to persecute the Christians of Damascus, to a faith that goes beyond mere theology and formulas and casts me into the mysterious but loving arms of God. I sometimes think that real faith means understanding less and less what is happening in my life and being more and more happy about it! The fact is that we control very little of what has real meaning in life but we can create the illusion of control and security by striving to manage at least the surface realities. Frequently, it takes some personal disaster to open our eyes to what is happening and, hopefully, to cast us into the arms of God. True and living faith will be marked by four characteristics: it will be grounded in the truth; it will trust the gift in life; it will lead to loving service and it will find expression in grateful prayer.

TRUE FAITH IS GROUNDED IN THE TRUTH

We have noted that biblical revelation is contained ultimately in the saving events described in the Bible. In order to receive this deeper revelation, we must in some way enter into those events; we must experience in some way the Exodus movement from bondage to freedom and the journey of Jesus from death to life. The chief obstacle to such an experience is self-delusion. The great saving events of the Bible are as real as real can be! Only those who enter into the reality of their own lives can establish vital contact with those supremely real events of salvation. If I do not like the life I have, I am tempted to take refuge from it in fantasy or illusion, but it is only in the life I have, in my real life, that I can find salvation. Actually, my life is far more interesting than I may think. But I must give it a chance by renouncing false goals and looking for the opportunity that is mine alone. Thus, the faith-response is grounded in the truth, in reality.

There is a story in the gospels which, if truly heard, should be very disconcerting.

At that time the disciples came to Jesus and asked, 'Who

is the greatest in the kingdom of Heaven?' He called a child, set him in front of them, and said, 'I tell you this: unless you turn round and become like children, you will never enter the kingdom of Heaven. Let a man humble himself till he is like this child, and he will be the greatest in the kingdom of Heaven' (Matt 18:1-4).

Jesus is speaking to his disciples who are not only adults but who already possess some measure of faith. But they, like many of us, still need to be further converted if they wish to be acceptable in the kingdom of God. It is clearly important to know how one can be "like this child."

In our Western culture, where children are often idealized, there is a tendency to think that being like a little child means being innocent or ingenuous. Since this seems impossible the text is dismissed as hopelessly idealistic. But this is not at all what Jesus meant. In the culture of his day, children were seen very realistically as weak and inexperienced and untested. Accordingly, though they were cherished, their opinions were given little consideration; they had little influence in the family circle. These "little ones," these powerless ones are held up by Jesus as models for Christians because, having no illusions about their ability to control life, they are quite content to accept it as a gift. In their case, control is so impossible that it becomes unimportant! Jesus hopes we will see that the only really important things in life are gifts that are well beyond our control; if we understand this we will be "like this child" — ready to receive the gift of the kingdom. To know this is to know the truth since real control of life, even for adults, is a foolish illusion.

The same teaching is found in the Beatitudes. Although Matthew gives us eight Beatitudes (5:3-10), scholars generally agree that only the four that he shares with Luke belong to the original group and that Luke's version is more ancient. It reads:

> How blest are you who are in need; the kingdom of God is yours. How blest are you who now go hungry; your hunger shall be satisfied. How blest are you who weep

> now; you shall laugh. How blest are you when men hate you, when they outlaw you and insult you, and ban your very name as infamous, because of the Son of man. On that day be glad and dance for joy; for assuredly you have a rich reward in heaven; in just the same way did their fathers treat the prophets (Luke 6:20-23).

The most important Beatitude is the first. The remaining Beatitudes simply add other dimensions to it. When Jesus declared the poor or needy blest, he was saying that they are to be congratulated, that they are the fortunate ones. Such a statement obviously contradicts the conventional wisdom which considers the poor and needy to be pitiful or cursed. The poor here are the ᶜanawim of the Old Testament: they were often destitute but that is not the primary meaning of the term. Rather, the emphasis is on their powerless condition; they are helpless, without influence, disregarded, easily overlooked. Jesus says that they should consider themselves fortunate, not because they are powerless, but because God has chosen them. God favors the weak and helpless. This does not mean of course that we should become doormats or obsessive dependents! What it does mean is that, in the matters that really count, we truly are helpless and must depend on God's love and goodness. If we are rich enough and talented enough to maintain the illusion of self-sufficiency, we are really unfortunate because we cannot then be open to the love of God. Relying too much on our own strength, we will not seek and receive the strength God offers us. This is surely what Paul meant when, having been converted from religious self-satisfaction, he wrote," . . . when I am weak, then I am strong" (2 Cor 12:10).

The hungry are called fortunate too, not because hunger in itself is good but because it is in fact the human condition to be hungering and yearning for fulfillment. To be human is to be incomplete, unfinished; it is to be away from home. Those who are filled with this world's goods may fail to discover how empty they are of what really counts. Blest then are those who dare to acknowledge their hunger and therefore seek the One who alone can satisfy them. These search the horizon for their true homeland and Jesus promises them that they shall not be disappointed.

Those who weep and mourn are also called fortunate. These are not the people who like to visit funeral parlors. They are rather those who cannot or choose not to insulate and protect themselves from the pain that comes from loving. To love as Jesus did is to become very vulnerable, to be exposed to hurt and sorrow. Those who embrace life in a loving way will indeed suffer much because of that but Jesus promises that they will be comforted in the end. This is not a reward for endurance but the wonderful fruit of an acceptance of life as God designed it, in its truth.

Finally, those are called fortunate who are misunderstood and ridiculed because they have chosen to live the ideals that Jesus taught. To relinquish freely and cheerfully the ambition for power and control will not be understood or applauded by a society that thrives on power and that measures success by the criterion of political or economic clout. Those for whom such dominance is not important will be considered strange and foolish. This does not mean that Christians should reject the responsibility of positions of power but they must not make the fatal mistake of seeing in that influence anything more than a means of love and service. They will be able to take power cheerfully and, more importantly, leave it gladly, for what really matters to them is the gift of love and their ability to love in turn because of that gift. That is the true opportunity in life; pursuit of power and control is the illusion in life. One's real life may seem threatening and demanding but it must be embraced because it is there alone that the gift is hidden.

FAITH TRUSTS THE GIFT IN LIFE

Faith begins with an overture from God. It may be an immediate experience of divine graciousness but it is more likely to be mediated through the love and kindness of another human being or even through the beauty and bounty of nature.

When this happens there is an experience of gift. The angels hold their breath to see what will happen next! For this gift can be received with caution or suspicion as if it were merely an accident, an exception to the general experience of competitive violence. Or it can be received as the promise and earnest of ever greater gift, in which case it becomes the first step in an adventure that leads to the discovery of the Gift of gifts.

The Bible teaches through story. When it wishes to express a profound truth, it shows us a person who represents that truth in the concrete reality of his or her life. Since the teaching is more important than the illustration, the author will not hesitate to embellish the historical reality so as to highlight the truth to be taught. The person becomes symbolic as well as historical. Thus the story of his or her life becomes the story of every believer. The critically important truth about faith as the discovery and trust of gift in life is illustrated in the story of King David.

Israel had a love affair with David. In her religious saga, he looms much larger than life. As Walter Brueggemann has noted:

> More than with any other person, Israel is fascinated by David, deeply attracted to him, bewildered by him, occasionally embarrassed by him, but never disowning him. David is one of those extraordinary historical figures who has a literary future. That is, his memory and presence keep generating more and more stories. One must, of course, recognize that others formulated those stories, perhaps even fabricated them. But surely there can be no doubt that it is David's magnificent and mysterious person that generated them, perhaps because Israel could never get it quite right. None of the stories quite comprehend him, let alone contain him (*David's Truth*, p.13).

David was indeed an historical king of Israel, reigning from 1000 to about 960 BCE. He captured Jerusalem and consolidated his kingdom around it before reaching out to annex surrounding nations. His empire represented the apex of Israel as a political entity. He was preceded by the ill-fated King Saul and followed by

King Solomon, whose tyrannical rule led to rebellion and schism. But we are interested here in the religious symbolism of David and, to appreciate that, we must look at Saul too for it seems evident that the biblical author intended that we should see in Saul the foil of David. David's significance is highlighted against the background of Saul.

King Saul, who had been chosen by Samuel to be Israel's first king, began his reign with great promise. He was an imposing figure, "a head taller than any of his fellows" (1 Sam 9:2), and he rallied the people to early victories over the Philistines. But a fatal flaw appeared and Samuel, who had chosen him for king, was quick to notice it. Saul had gathered his small army at Gilgal and was waiting for Samuel to come to offer sacrifice so that God might support them in battle. After waiting in vain for seven days, Saul, in desperation, offered the sacrifice himself. No sooner done than Samuel appeared, scolding him for usurping the priest's office and declaring ominously that another would be found to take his place (1 Sam 13:3-14).

Samuel's reaction far exceeded the gravity of Saul's offense. It seems in fact that what Samuel found most reprehensible in Saul was not his well-intentioned mistake but his failure to act like a king, including perhaps his failure to reject Samuel's criticism! After all, Samuel's tardiness was the real fault of that day. When Saul later failed to carry out the letter of Samuel's order to destroy the Amalekites, one sees even more clearly the deep insecurity of Saul as he begged for a second chance (1 Sam 15). Samuel must have been disheartened to see the king of Israel whimpering in this fashion.

It would be interesting and revealing to wonder what David would have done in such a situation. For David was as self-confident and decisive as Saul was insecure and wavering. David had no liturgical scruples when he and his men took and ate the sacred bread (1 Sam 21:3-6). David also committed really serious sins, notably when he ordered the death of Uriah to cover up his sin with Bathsheba (2 Sam 11). But he was able to repent and seemed to be even better for the experience. Saul managed to turn peccadillos into unforgivable sins; David turned grievous sins into opportunities for grace and growth. Saul was snake-bitten, always in the wrong line of traffic, forever snatching defeat from the jaws of victory! David, by contrast, had a golden touch, won out against all odds, always seemed to know exactly the right thing to say or do.

At first sight, it seems that David was lucky and Saul was cursed. But David knew adversity too: the incest against Tamar, the murder of Amnon, the treason of Absalom, the disobedience of Joab. The difference goes much deeper than chance. It is a matter of faith. Saul and David both believed in God and in the goodness of God. But Saul, unlike David, seemed incapable of believing in the goodness of God's world, of God's future and of Saul himself. And so he was a worried, anxious man and was always prepared for evil and almost always found it. David was confident, optimistic, positive; he was prepared for good, for happy surprise and, since God's world is basically good, he was able to find blessing, in spite of problems and setbacks. Saul could not lead Israel, as Samuel sensed, because no one will follow a loser. David was an extraordinary leader because he was ready to see the promise in others and trusted his own instincts in bringing that promise to fruition.

Most of all, David trusted God and life and himself enough to be able to do the risky, marginal things which are the hallmark of the truly free person. He "danced without restraint" as he led the Ark of the Covenant up to Jerusalem (2 Sam 6:14). When his wife Michal (Saul's daughter) criticized him, he replied simply, "Before the Lord I will dance for joy . . ." (2 Sam 6:21). Before the Lord, David dared to be himself, to follow his instincts, to celebrate the good in life and to let the evil pass.

But the most dramatic example of the effect of David's faith was his battle with the giant, Goliath (1 Sam 17:12-54). David was too young to be a soldier but his father sent him to see how his brothers were faring in the campaign of Saul against the Philistines. David found Goliath there before Israel, hurling insults and challenging Saul and his men to fight him. No one could be found for this hopeless contest with the giant. Then David stepped forward. They were dumbfounded but they were also desperate so they accepted his offer. Then Saul did a very characteristic thing: he offered David his own suit of armor though it was clearly much too large. Even at this point, Saul could think of only one way to fight the giant — the traditional way, the old way, the doomed way. David saw the new and better way and as soon as he decided to fight Goliath with his sling the battle was as good as over. Thus, David's faith, since it revealed the goodness of God in life, put him in touch with his own creativity as well. He became imaginative and innovative. David did not conquer Goliath because God intervened; he killed the giant because his trust in God enabled him to trust himself, to make the most of the talents and ingenuity that God had given him. It has been said: Saul looked at Goliath and said, "How big he is; how can I fight him?" But David looked at Goliath and said, "How big he is; how can I miss him?"

David is therefore much more than an historical person; he is also a model and type of the authentic believer. True faith liberates and every true believer will be, in some sense, a positive David-figure. But no one is so perfect a believer that he does not also have Saul lurking deep inside him — tempting him to be suspicious, to be critical and negative, to blame others for all his problems. If one does not consciously choose to be David and to reject Saul, there is always the danger of slipping into bitterness and being overcome by evil. In the movie, "Amadeus," Salieri is a Saul-figure: he has a beautiful gift but he cannot enjoy it or make the most of it because he must constantly compare it to the genius of Mozart. This is truly a matter of life and death, for Saul ended a suicide and David became the model for the Messiah. In the New Testament, Jesus is "son of David" but not just because he is in David's line; he is the perfect David-figure, standing up to the Goliath of death-dealing sin, armed not with traditional power but with the new power of love, and winning the ultimate victory.

TRUE FAITH LEADS TO LOVING SERVICE

God's loving choice of Israel involved a moral imperative that set her people apart from other nations. They were to be different from the Gentiles, not only because they were uniquely loved but also because they were expected to respond to that love with a higher standard of moral behavior. This challenge to Israel was based in part upon the fact that God's revelation to her enabled her to see and understand the meaning and purpose of human life with a clarity that the Gentiles, having only natural revelation, could never achieve. Moses had noted this: "What great nation has a god close at hand as the Lord our God is close to us whenever we call to him? What great nation is there whose statutes and laws are just, as is all this law which I am setting before you today?" (Deut 4:7-8).

Clearer revelation, however, is no guarantee of more ethical behavior, as Paul would point out later to the Romans: "For (again from Scripture) 'no human being can be justified in the sight of God' for having kept the law: law brings only the consciousness of sin" (3:20). One may know what should be done but not be sufficiently motivated to do it; or one may do what is right for wrong motives. T.S. Eliot has Becket say when he is thinking of the glories of martyrdom: "The last temptation is the greatest treason: To do the right deed for the wrong reason" (*Murder in the Cathedral,* p. 44). That is why Paul points out the severe limitations of mere knowledge of what is right or wrong. One needs more than a road map to reach one's destination.

The secret of properly motivated moral behavior is found in the very act by which one receives the freedom that makes moral behavior possible. True freedom comes only from love; it was God's love, experienced by the slaves, that made the Exodus possible. But to receive freedom from being loved is to know instinctively the purpose of that freedom: it is for loving others into freedom. Suddenly, it becomes clear that, just as only love can give true freedom, so also the only proper use of freedom is to love others and thereby to continue the liberating process.

The freedom and confidence that come to me because I am loved thus become the source of my own ability and opportunity for loving. In this way, love and freedom become part of a wonderful widening circle of goodness and salvation. Where love is lacking and freedom must be "stolen" its true purpose will be obscured and it may become a freedom for violence and control rather than for love and liberation.

The Bible frequently dwells on this important point and it does so usually in a very concrete way. Thus, the author of Deuteronomy, advising Israel about proper behavior among God's liberated people, writes:

> You shall not deprive aliens and orphans of justice nor take a widow's cloak in pledge. Remember that you were slaves in Egypt and the Lord your God redeemed you from there; that is why I command you to do this (Deut 24:17-18).

This golden text, when translated into contemporary idiom, clearly establishes the basis for morality, not only in Israel but for the whole Bible. The alien, orphan and widow represent defenseless and vulnerable people — the orphan and widow for obvious reasons and the alien because, in clan society, one's only protection was the clan-brothers and they are not available when one travels away from one's home. Israel, in her strength and freedom, must at all cost resist the temptation to take advantage of the weakness of others. If she replies, "But everyone does it!", God's answer is: "Remember that you were slaves in Egypt; remember that you were not always strong and secure and beautiful; remember that I loved you when you were weak and frightened and unattractive; remember how you received your present strength and freedom and, above all, do not ever forget what that means! It means that you must henceforth use all the freedom that you have as you experienced my use of freedom, that is, as a means for loving and freeing and strengthening others."

This is the radical moral imperative of biblical revelation. Jesus gave it a wonderful new expression but he did not change it.

Having been affirmed into freedom by his Father, he converted that freedom into love, service and sacrifice — to the end. As beneficiaries of that love, expressed in our lives by all those who truly love us, we too must use the resulting freedom and confidence to affirm and care for those not yet as free as we are. We must resist the temptation to exercise psychic control over those who may be less secure. We must remember that what security we feel (and it too is limited) has been the free gift of someone's love, bringing with it the responsibility to use it to build up and not to put down. This is precisely what we read in 1 John 3:16: "It is by this that we know what love is: that Christ laid down his life for us. And we in our turn are bound to lay down our lives for our brothers."And again in 1 John 4:11: "If God thus loved us, dear friends, we in turn are bound to love one another." But we must always remember that it is not enough to have heard about the love of God; it must be experienced, and the primary task of any faith community is to see that its members truly experience God's love. Only when that is assured can there be reminders of duties and responsibilities.

This reminds us of the tremendous gap that exists between moral and merely legal behavior. Many persons who are charged and convicted of crimes have experienced so little love in their lives that they have found it almost impossible to avoid violence. This does not excuse their behavior and society certainly needs to be protected from their violent tendencies. But God knows who might have given them love and did not. Many smug, judgmental and upstanding citizens may have to share in the guilt for crimes when all the facts are known. Those who have been blest with talent, opportunity and love must constantly examine their consciences concerning their attitude toward the "aliens, orphans and widows" in their lives. It would not be farfetched to guess that the first question asked on the day of judgment will be: "Did you let my people go?" For we must account for the use of the freedom that has been given to us: do we use it as Pharaoh did — to dominate, to control, to enslave? or do we use it as God did — to love, to liberate, to create? Only after we have been judged on the answers to those questions will there be further inquiries about such secondary matters as keeping rules. For it is a simple fact that, though observing laws is important, it can never be as important as giving or preserving life!

FAITH-INSPIRED PRAYER

The biblical stories about David tell of his political and military exploits. It is a little surprising then to discover that Israel's prayer book, the 150 Psalms, was attributed to David. And this fact is not lost on Christian sculptors and artists who show David more frequently with a harp than with a sword. It is well known, of course, that most of the Psalms were written long after David and this was certainly known by those who first called it David's Psalter. They were not trying to deceive us. This was their way of emphasizing a very important feature of the Psalms, namely, that they were all written by and express the attitudes of a David-figure. David's positive faith must always burst forth in grateful prayer and the Psalms provide an ideal expression of that David-spirit. Small wonder that it has been the classic prayerbook of both Jews and Christians.

There is a wonderful variety among the Psalms. They reflect the whole spectrum of human experience, particularly as it relates to God. Human misery and fear and anguish are fully explored but the one constant feature is a deep and abiding conviction about the reality and presence and goodness of God. The Psalms celebrate the goodness that faith discovers in life. There are petitions for help, of course, but they too are a form of praise because one does not ask help from God if he is not thought to be good and caring. But most of the Psalms are various expressions of the classic Jewish berakah or thanksgiving. In its simplest form, this prayer begins: "Blessed art thou, Lord our God, king of the universe. . ." followed by the reason for the praise and thanksgiving. Frequently, God is praised for ambiguous or mysterious realities. This reflects a David-like conviction that it is goodness, not evil, that is hidden in the mysterious events of life.

As faith becomes stronger it is possible to praise God for ever more mysterious realities in life. This has the effect of releasing their hidden goodness which would otherwise go unnoticed, leaving only the darkness of the mystery. Thus, one who is gradually transformed by praying the Psalms will be able to bless the interruptions and disruptions in life. This will enable him to welcome God whose coming is almost always unexpected. It frequently occurs that what appeared at first to be a troublesome distraction will, if blest, turn out to be a happy surprise.

I was preaching once about this kind of prayer when a dog began to bark loudly outside the chapel. I could see that I was losing the attention of my audience and was about to conclude my homily in frustration when I realized that the barking dog, if blest, could be turned from enemy to ally. So I raised my voice slightly and said, "In other words, we must learn in life to bless everything, even barking dogs!" The dog stopped barking at that moment, which led me to wonder whether it, like so many creatures, was not perhaps being disruptive because it had never been blest!

As one's trust in the hidden goodness of life becomes stronger, it will be possible to bless more and more of life's ambiguities. It takes no special faith to be grateful for obvious good things like vacation for a schoolboy or sunshine for a picnic; even pagans know that these things are good. But the believer will thank God for ever more ambiguous realities until there is nothing for which he cannot be grateful. He will thank God for the new day before he checks the weather or thinks about its burdens. This will allow the day's goodness to have a chance to show itself. It is said that Pope John XXIII was speaking one day to a group of seminarians in Rome. He was fully aware that his cancer was terminal, yet he said: "Every day is a good day — a good day for living, and a good day for dying." It seems to me that this ability to call the imminent day of death a good day derived from Pope John's lifelong habit of calling every day good because it was a gift from God. He thus became in a sense a victim of that habit so that as the dark day of dying approached he found that he could do only what he had always done and blessed it too. Surely Pope John's daily recitation of the Psalms in his breviary must have been an important factor in the development of such a pervasive sense of prayerfulness.

It is important not to be selective when praying the Psalms. There is a real danger in avoiding Psalms (or any biblical texts) that do not appeal to us. A religion built only on "favorite texts" is likely to be a religion that accommodates our prejudices rather than corrects them and converts us. Some people have a special problem with the so-called cursing Psalms. Psalm 109 is a good example of this type. But we should not claim too quickly that the sentiments expressed there are completely foreign to us, for we too can be vengeful at times and this Psalm provides an opportunity to recognize that and to place it before the Lord for correction.

In the Sayings of the Desert Fathers there is a story about a fervent young monk who went to one of the Fathers with a problem about his prayer life. He told the wise old man that he found it very difficult to say the positive Psalms on days when he was feeling low. He wondered if it would not be better to divide the Psalter and to say the 75 generally upbeat Psalms twice on his good days and the other 75 Psalms twice on his bad days, thus still saying the required 150 Psalms each day. The wise old man told him that that was precisely what he should not do. For the praying of the Psalms is meant to remind us of joyful events when we are sad and of tragedies when we are exuberant so that we may be taken out of our private little world and may become aware of others and of their joys and hardships. Thus, the Psalms will bring equilibrium and harmony into our chaotic lives.

For the Christian, the ultimate and most perfect praising of God is the Eucharist, which is a name derived directly from the Hebrew word *berakah*. In the Eucharistic liturgy, Jesus praises his Father for his goodness and mercy. He does so by proclaiming that goodness but also, and more effectively, by becoming himself a perfect sign of trust as he gives up his life in response to his

Father's request. When we participate in the Eucharist, we join Jesus in praising the Father; we bring all the *berakahs* that we have been able to say in the ups and downs of life and we add them to this central *berakah* that we offer with Jesus. If we have not been trying to bless both the bitter and the sweet in our lives, we will find it difficult to enter truly into the mystery of the Eucharist. When we see Jesus praising the Father for the opportunity to endure humiliation and to let his body be broken and his blood poured out for our sake, we will more readily understand the sacrifices that Christian living and loving require of us.

Our commitment to embrace the sacrifices of loving service is confirmed by our reception of the sacrificed Body and Blood of the Lord. As Saint Paul pointed out in his letter to the community at Corinth (1 Cor 11:16-34), there can be sincere and fruitful reception of the Eucharist only where people truly care for each other. Those who think only of their own needs and interests cannot be truly joined to the Body that is broken and the Blood that is poured out in love and concern for others. Thus, the Sacrament of the Eucharist is not just the sign of the Lord's presence; most of all, it is the sign of the Lord's love, and thus it is a constant reminder of the true purpose of human life.

SIN AS FAILURE TO RESPOND TO LOVE

Many people complain that they are not loved enough and they may excuse themselves from responsibility because of this. Their insight is accurate, for those who are not loved cannot be free and thus cannot assume responsibility. However, it is very unlikely that they have not been loved at all and the real question is, how have they responded to the love that was available? No one is loved perfectly and therefore one can always find excuses. The determination of sinfulness will hinge ultimately upon one's response to the love in one's life. This must of course be true love that seeks our good and our freedom. If we squander that gift, we commit sin, and the degree of our guilt will be commensurate with the gift that is offered to us. This sinfulness can therefore be classified as the opposite of the kinds of faith response listed above: it can be failure in truthfulness, in trusting, in loving service and in gratitude.

We fail in truthfulness when we indulge in day-dreaming. It is true that, when there is not much love or appreciation in our lives, we may find it almost impossible to struggle against the negative forces. When our lives are filled with constant reminders of our inadequacies or with tasks that are not rewarding we will be sorely tempted to take refuge in the more congenial world of daydreaming. But this cotton candy world has no real nourishment in it. My confrere, Campion Gavaler, has written:

> The conditions which bring on daydreaming are about the same as those which bring on the ultimate escape from reality, suicide: namely, the feeling of not being appreciated, the feeling that life is empty, the feeling of inadequacy. The person who daydreams seeks to escape his limitations not within the slow course of life with its partial successes, but in the more controllable and immediately gratifying world of fantasy (unpublished essay).

Daydreaming becomes sinful when it distrusts and rejects the world that God has provided for a world of one's own making. It is destructive because it wastes the opportunity to find love and freedom in the only world that offers them, in the real world. This real world may seem unpromising but it is precisely the task of faith to discover hidden opportunities and blessings. Some of the most exquisite flowers bloom in the desert.

The original sin of Adam and Eve was of course a sin of pride since they refused to accept their assigned status as creatures subject to God's determination of right and wrong. Attempts have been made to be more specific about the nature of that sin. My own suggestion would be that the special kind of pride expressed is that attitude which refuses to look for opportunity in the imperfect world in which we find ourselves and opts instead for an escape through complaints and excuses. When challenged by God, Adam blamed Eve, who in turn blamed the serpent. To turn to excuses and blaming others instead of looking for good and doing one's best may well be the original, i.e., the universal sin.

The sinfulness that distrusts life is illustrated by the tragic life of King Saul. He found evil and darkness in his life, as all do, but he allowed it to gain the upper hand and to cast a blight eventually on everything he did. This is usually a gradual process. It begins with a tendency to be critical and judgmental which becomes ever more pervasive until it darkens everything. Nothing is beyond criticism; everything is flawed. The final stage in this process is bitterness which drives all enjoyment out of life and makes happy surprises impossible. The two biblical figures who personified this tragic destiny were Saul and Judas. Both were talented and showed great promise but they were both consumed by darkness and ended in suicide. The Saul-figure may not actually commit suicide but his rejection of the life-giving power to choose light and goodness results in a living death.

The sinfulness that rejects loving service is often, like fantasizing and negativity, a defensive kind of behavior. It takes refuge in selfishness because it does not feel free enough and strong enough to reach out to others. Because of a basic insecurity, it wastes much precious time in selfish preoccupation with survival in a supposedly hostile world. This kind of attitude is sinful to the degree that the insecurity is the result of choosing not to accept the love and affirmation that are available. Some are insecure through no fault of their own and all are insecure at times. But one sins when that insecurity is perpetuated through a deliberate refusal to trust the signs of goodness in life.

There is another kind of selfishness which is more pernicious. This is the introverted attitude of those who have forgotten that their freedom and strength are gifts. They disregard the warning of Deut 24:17 about care for the weak and vulnerable ones. Since they wrongly believe that their freedom is their own achievement, they indulge in it as if it did not imply serious responsibilities. They easily excuse themselves from any obligation toward the less fortunate and less sophisticated members of society, unfairly attributing their misfortune to laziness and callously suggesting that the better things in life would be wasted on them. Since these are usually the relatively free and affluent and educated people, they can readily rationalize their insensitivity, but God knows their responsibility and will demand an accounting. Isaiah sounds a frequent prophetic warning when he writes:

> Though you offer countless prayers, I will not listen. There is blood on your hands; wash yourselves and be clean . . . Cease to do evil and learn to do right, pursue justice and champion the oppressed; give the orphan his rights, plead the widow's cause (1:15-17).

Just as berakah-prayer and Eucharist are celebrations of the wonderful gifts that faith discovers in human life, so is ingratitude a deadly form of sinfulness. It is often instructive to compare the different ways that people talk about their educational experiences. Those who have a healthy, positive attitude toward life usually speak in grateful and glowing terms about their teachers. By contrast, negative and critical people can only find fault with those who taught them. The fact is that they all very probably had the usual proportion of good, bad and indifferent teachers. Once again, one must decide whether the past is to be used as an excuse for present failings or as cause for grateful remembrance.

Dag Hammarskjöld has written, "For all that has been — Thanks! To all that shall be — Yes!" (*Markings*, p.89). One cannot be truly open to the future and ready to see its opportunities if he is not at peace with his past. Perhaps one could amend Hammarskjöld's statement by saying, "Thanks for as much as possible of the past and forgiveness for the rest; then a resounding Yes to all that will be." It is sinful to nurse past injuries, real or imagined; and it is also destructive, for it denies one access to the future as prepared by God.

Part Two:

The Adventure

4
The Journey

We have already noted that the entire Old Testament is centered in the event of Exodus. God's liberation of his people from bondage was an act of creation; a new people was constituted and set on a journey. From that moment until the end of time Israel will be a traveling people, for they live in promise and yearn for fulfillment. This was dramatically represented in the Passover ritual which Moses prescribed for the people the night before they were to leave Egypt.

PASSOVER: A COMMITMENT TO JOURNEY

In this Passover ritual a yearling lamb or kid was to be chosen. In the evening before the first full moon after the spring equinox, the animal was to be slaughtered.

> They must take some of the blood and smear it on the two doorposts and on the lintel of every house in which they eat the lamb. On that night they shall eat the flesh roast on the fire; they shall eat it with unleavened cakes and bitter herbs . . . This is the way in which you must eat it; you shall have your belt fastened, your sandals on your feet and your staff in your hand, and you must eat in urgent haste. It is the Lord's Passover (Exod 12:7-11).

It is clear that this sacrifice of the paschal lamb was made to God and, like all such sacrifices, was intended to express Israel's total dependence on God. The lamb is a surrogate or substitute for the people. Since human sacrifice was forbidden, a lamb was offered instead. In the circumstances of the Exodus, when they were about to defy the power of the Pharaoh, this sacrifice was Israel's way of putting herself entirely into the hands of God. They were saying, in effect: "We dare to undertake this humanly impossible adventure because of the hope that you have given us."

In order to appreciate more fully the implications of this dramatic ritual, it is important to realize that it was almost certainly borrowed in large part from a pre-existing ritual used by shepherds to assure the protection of their flocks as they broke winter camp. Among the semi-nomadic tribes of the ancient Near East, it was necessary to spend the summer months, when there was little or no rainfall, in a constant search for new pasture for the flocks of sheep and goats. This meant that every spring they would have to leave the relative safety of their winter camps with their protective enclosures to begin the dangerous summer journeying when the flocks would be exposed to wild animals and other hazards. To involve the protection of their gods, they would offer sacrifice and then smear the blood of the sacrifice on their tents to ward off the evil spirits who might harm their flocks. They ate the sacrifice in the nomad way, roasted and with unleavened bread and bitter herbs.

Israel saw that this springtime sacrifice of their ancestors was most appropriate for their own situation. For they too were leaving a place that represented a certain kind of safety but where there was also inevitable death for them as a people. And they were moving into an unknown, uncharted world with all the terrors that that prospect implied. It is not surprising then that they should have adopted the ancient nomadic ritual, retaining many of its features but purging it of its pagan implications. Thus, they stamped forever on the Passover sacrifice the significance of departure from a seemingly safe but truly fatal attachment to the familiar past and movement into a seemingly dangerous but truly life-giving commitment to the mystery of God's future.

In this context, the description of the manner in which the Passover meal was to be eaten becomes powerfully symbolic: ". . . you shall have your belt fastened" (to hold up the long garb and free the feet and legs for travel), "your sandals on your feet""(as protection on the rocky, unfamiliar terrain), "and your staff in your hand" (to fend off dangerous animals), "and you must eat it in urgent haste" (as one eager for the journey) (Exod 12:11). This picture is like a frame in a motion picture that is frozen because of its special significance. This is what a true Israelite must be: one ready and eager for the journey from the bondage of the past with its dangerous human attractions, to freedom in the future with its challenging divine promise!

We will never be able to understand the Bible if we do not sense this dynamic and fluid quality that pervades the biblical concept of reality. The great German scholar, Gerhard von Rad, has stated it succinctly:

> Here (in Israel) everything is in motion, the accounts never balance, and fulfillment unexpectedly gives rise in turn to another promise of something greater still. Here nothing has its ultimate meaning in itself, but is always an earnest of something still greater (Quoted by J. Moltmann in *Religion, Revolution and the Future*, p. 29).

Everything is under the seal of promise: God has liberated his people but he has liberated them for journey, not for rest. As von Rad has noted, there are little fulfillments, but only to establish the basis for hope and to set the stage for new promise and new challenge. The empire of David was proof of God's favor but it disappeared and left an aching void filled only with hope and yearning for a new David and a Messianic kingdom. The miracles of Jesus in Galilee seemed to announce that final kingdom but they too ceased and left a yearning for the great and final miracles of Resurrection and the Second Coming. We too experience the early "miracles" as we discover love, freedom and strength in our lives but our strength wanes and we are challenged to live in hope of personal resurrection.

Thus, the Bible instructs us about the fact of human impermanence. God has made us incomplete. When we feel the pain of that emptiness we are in touch with reality, we are living in the truth. This becomes a problem only if we turn to material or merely human comforts to fill the void. Such things will never suffice since the aching and yearning is for God; only the Creator can complete what is lacking in his creatures. This is the restlessness, the painful yearning that Saint Augustine wrote about: "My soul is restless, 0 Lord, until it rests in Thee" (*Confessions,* 1,1). Jürgen Moltmann writes in a similar vein: "It is from promise that there arises that element of unrest which allows of no coming to terms with a present that is unfulfilled" (*The Theology of Hope,* p. 102). The journey of Israel and of the disciples of Jesus is therefore a bitter-sweet adventure: a present painful experience of longing but an horizon that is illuminated with the glow of divine promise.

"COME AND SEE" (JOHN 1:38)

In John's version of the call of the first disciples, we read that two of them were following Jesus. "When he turned and saw them following him, he asked, 'What are you looking for?' They said, 'Rabbi' (which means a teacher), 'where are you staying?' 'Come and see,' he replied" (John 1:38). In view of John's love for symbolism, it would be a mistake to see this simply as a friendly exchange. Rather, the question of Jesus implies that he perceives in them (and in us) that deep longing that is characteristic of humans when they allow themselves to be in touch with their true condition. It is as if he had said, "Why, you must be earthlings, for I see that you are searching for something!" The disciples call him "Rabbi" because they sense that if he knows their innermost yearning, he must also know where to find what they seek; he must be a teacher of truth. So they ask him, "Where are you staying?"

They are certainly not asking him for his address. Their question means, "Where can we find you and learn from you about our true home?" Jesus says, in reply, "Come and see." He does not give a pat answer; he offers instead an invitation to walk with him and to learn what living in hope means, what the journey means — to learn of its pain but also of its joy, and most of all of its happy ending, its true homecoming.

This ability to live in hope may very well be the single most distinctive characteristic of the biblical person as opposed to the devotee of secular philosophy. From the secular perspective, everything must make sense here and now; human success and happiness must be found in this life. Hence the need to seek immediate fulfillment. Time is an enemy, especially as one grows older, for it erodes relentlessly the opportunity for present enjoyment. From the biblical perspective, it is promise that dominates and true fulfillment is reserved for the end of life. The only real concern during life is to assure that one has chosen the path that leads to that homeland. This is not an easy path; it puts aside personal gratification for the good of others; it is the Jesus-path of loving care and sacrifice. From this perspective, the length of life is not a major concern because one step in the right direction is as good as a thousand. This provides freedom from excessive anxiety or angry frustration; it also means an old age that is not just meaningless and helpless waiting for death but rather joyful expectation as one looks forward eagerly for the arrival at home. The fact that perhaps only a few can claim this experience is simply proof that we need to be more fully converted from the infection of secular philosophy to the bright hope of biblical revelation.

THE "WILDERNESS" OF DIVINE MYSTERY

The words that best summarize the Exodus experience are found in Exodus 5:1: "After this, Moses and Aaron came to Pharaoh and said, 'These are the words of the Lord the God of Israel:

'Let my people go so that they may keep my pilgrim-feast in the wilderness.' " It is true, of course, that the most important words in that message from God are the words commanding Pharaoh to liberate the chosen people. But the words that complete that command must not be overlooked. At first glance, one might dismiss them as no more than a general reference to the relatively unknown land beyond Egypt's borders and to the excuse for seeking freedom. But that would ignore the special importance of the word "wilderness" in Israel's religious history.

Wilderness translates the Hebrew word, *midbar,* which is sometimes incorrectly translated as "desert." The Hebrew dictionary tells us that midbar means:

(a) tracts of land, used for pastorage of flocks and herds;
(b) uninhabited land

The word conveys therefore the sense of a land that is still wide open space, unsurveyed, unmapped, undomesticated by man. It is land that is still relatively free of human control. In the context of Exodus it stands in sharp contrast to Egypt which was very much under human control. In fact, the Egypt of the Pharaohs was famous for its order and neatness. It is important to emphasize this contrast because the wilderness came to symbolize in Israel's tradition the mystery of God. Egypt represented human rationality, human order — and slavery. The wilderness represented divine presence, the freedom of God, lack of human control — and freedom.

Therefore, when God commanded Pharaoh to let his people go so that they might keep his pilgrim-feast in the wilderness, he had in mind nothing less than the destiny of that people. Their task in history would be henceforth to move resolutely through time, entertaining the presence of God and honoring the ideals of the Exodus in their lives. This amounts to living in mystery because the selflessness of those ideals will appear foolish to human reason and logic. To be foolishly unselfish will be to live in the wilderness, in mystery, in God's country!

It may be noted in passing that those who clamor for "law and order" as a solution to all the problems of human society should reflect upon the strange fact that the law and order of Egypt (and of many modern oppressive societies) produced slavery for most of its inhabitants. We must always ask a question here: Whose law and order do you have in mind? Usually it is only the law and order of the powerful elite which effectively prevent the reforms that would give justice to others. There is, of course, an authentic and praiseworthy law and order but it is the law and order of God whereby the rights of all are honored. It will probably never be quite as neat and logical as tyrannical law and order because it needs to satisfy so many but it will have the great merit of assuring a real sense of justice and freedom. Under dictators, trains and buses are more likely to run on time but the people in them are less likely to be smiling!

There is another important dimension to the wilderness symbolism. In Hebrew thought, the dynamic mode is primary. History is experienced as linear, not cyclical: it is launched by creation and moves relentlessly toward consummation. Individuals are born into that flow and are called to shape it by their decisions. We have already noted Emil Brunner's remark about the primacy of the verb over the substantive in Hebrew thought (p. 23). This emphasis on the action word is clearly illustrated by the fact that, in the Hebrew declaratory sentence, the verb precedes the subject. Thus, for example, the first sentence of the Bible reads literally: "In the beginning created God the heavens and the earth." This primary concern for the temporal and dynamic aspects of life caused the Bible to see the wilderness not only as a symbol of divine mystery but also as a symbol of the future. The unknown future is in a special sense God's preserve. God gives it to us and we accept it from his hand. If we do not know or trust God's goodness, the future is threatening and forbidding and the past, with its known and familiar aspects, becomes a refuge. When Israel was called out of Egypt, she was also called out of the past and asked to move joyfully and trustingly into God's future. To keep God's pilgrim-feast in the wilderness then means to entertain divine mystery and to move eagerly and hopefully into the future, including especially the end of human life.

The Israelites spent forty years in the Sinai wilderness. Forty years were considered to be one generation, one typical lifetime. Like every human life, it began with a call into being and freedom and was meant to end, after a time of testing, with entrance into the Promised Land, the land flowing with milk and honey. The testing involved three questions: Can God's people, having experienced his love for them, endure a period of emptiness and unfulfillment? Can God's people resist the temptation to go back to the familiar but fatal past? Can God's people maintain hope of a happy ending in spite of reports about humanly insurmountable obstacles ahead?

The Israelites did not fare well in this test of their loyalty. Though God sent them journey-bread (manna), they continued to complain bitterly so that Moses was exasperated (Numbers 11:10-15). They begged to be allowed to return to Egypt: "Think of it! In Egypt we had fish for the asking, cucumbers and watermelons, leeks and onions and garlic" (Num 11:5). Of course, there was no hope in Egypt, but even prison can seem good to those who fear the unknown. Finally, the scouts returned from Canaan and reported that, though it was indeed a land of milk and honey, it was defended by giants and so was beyond their reach. "Then the whole Israelite community cried out in dismay; all night long they wept" (Num 14:1).

Moses tried to reassure them, "You need not fear the people of the land . . . They have lost the protection they had: the Lord is with us. You have nothing to fear from them" (Num 14:9). But human rationality won out over the witness of faith: ". . . by way of answer the assembled Israelites threatened to stone them" (Num 14:10). God said to Moses: "How much longer will they refuse to trust me in spite of all the signs I have shown among them?" (Num 14:11). We should note that God was angry because they had forgotten his goodness to them in the past. Hence, his sentence against them: "Not one of all those who have seen my glory and the signs which I wrought in Egypt and in the wilderness shall see the country which I promised on oath to their fathers" (Num 14:22-23).

It is not difficult to see that this testing of Israel in the wilderness of Sinai was a prototype of the testing of all believers. Believers of all ages are asked to endure the aching void of incompleteness as they care for others and look ahead to a distant homeland. There will be adequate nourishment in the manna of hope and in the genuine satisfaction of a clear conscience but there will also be the anguish of aloneness and the ever present temptation to fill the void reserved for God with material distractions or merely human love. This is the time of fidelity and perseverance, the virtues that gradually change the untested generosity of youth into the profound readiness and joy of the mature Christian. Believers are also asked to resist the strong temptation to turn away from the unknown and threatening future to take refuge in the past with its little victories and its familiar features. It is relatively easy to look ahead when one is young and full of zest for life. But when the subtle but unmistakable hints of decline appear, there is grave danger that one will gradually turn more and more toward the past. There will be more consolation and comfort in the scrapbook than in the threatening future! However, to muse about the "good old days" is to quit the journey and to die.

Finally, and worst of all, believers are tempted to distrust God's promise of true freedom and happiness at the end of the journey as they listen to the woeful predictions of the prophets of doom who, like those scouts returning from Canaan with stories of impregnable cities and fierce giants, will point out the terrors of old age, dependence, suffering and death. The antidote to this poisonous message is the remembrance of God's love and mercy in the past and the firm conviction of his fidelity to the promises and of incredible victory in the end.

In view of the profound symbolism of the wilderness journey of Israel, it is not surprising that it was recalled in Psalm 95: "Do not grow stubborn as you were at Meribah, as at the time of Massah in the wilderness, when your forefathers challenged me

... For forty years I was indignant with that generation ..."
(Ps 95:8-10). The application of this Psalm to the wilderness
journey of believers is made explicitly by the author of the letter
to the Hebrews:

> And with whom was God indignant for forty years?
> With those, surely, who had sinned, whose bodies lay
> where they fell in the desert. And to whom did he vow
> that they should not enter his rest, if not to those who
> had refused to believe? We perceive that it was unbelief
> which prevented their entering (3:17-19).

Small wonder then that Psalm 95 became the Invitatory Psalm
at the beginning of daily Matins for all those who, through the
ages, have prayed the Divine Office. To follow Jesus is to become a
friend of mystery, one who makes his way through the wilderness,
cheerfully, joyfully, expectantly — picking desert flowers and
watching the horizon!

ENTERTAINING DIVINE MYSTERY IN HOSPITALITY

We have said that the wilderness of Sinai symbolized divine
mystery. It is important to note the special meaning of mystery in
this context. Frequently, mystery is thought to be simply some-thing
obscure, impenetrable, unknown — as in mystery novels or the
expression, "It's a mystery to me." When we speak of divine mystery,
certainly the element of the unknown or unfathomable is present
also but, in this case, though the mystery may be beyond human
comprehension it is not therefore meaningless, much less irrelevant.
In fact, since humans were created to become recipients of
divine presence, nothing that they can understand will ever be as
meaningful to them as is divine mystery. God's mystery is the fire
in the cloud; it cannot be penetrated and controlled but it contains
the meaning of everything!
To make room in one's life for the reality, and therefore the

mystery, of God is to practice a special form of hospitality. In fact, this openness to divine presence is often illustrated in the Bible by stories in which strangers are entertained. No doubt the best known of these stories is found in Genesis where Abraham is pictured showing hospitality to the three strangers who came to him as he was dwelling with Sarah by the oaks of Mamre (Gen 18:1-15). Mamre, in southern Palestine, was the end of a long journey for Abraham. He pulled up his roots and left Ur in Mesopotamia because God called him even though he was already seventy-five years old. And his destination was described simply as "a country that I will show you" (Gen 12:1). Abraham "set out as the Lord had bidden him" (Gen 12:4), trusting completely in the promise of God that, though he and Sarah were childless, he would eventually have descendants as "countless as the dust of the earth" (Gen 13:16). Thus, Abraham lived with mystery as he trusted in and acted on a humanly incredible promise.

By the time Abraham and Sarah came to Mamre, they had "grown very old, and Sarah was past the age of child-bearing" (Gen 18:11). In fact, Abraham was about a hundred years old (Gen 21:5) and Sarah was a relatively youthful ninety! The Bible emphasizes (perhaps even exaggerates) the advanced age of this couple to highlight the folly, from a merely human and rational perspective, of continued hope that God would in fact be faithful to his glowing promises. Thus the bleak and childless old age of Abraham and Sarah stand in sharp contrast to the repeated and extravagant divine promises of numberless posterity.

Abraham's morose meditation on unfulfilled promises was suddenly interrupted by the appearance on the horizon of three strangers! (I am always tempted to supplement the biblical text at this point to guess that Abraham was ready to tell Sarah to pull the blinds and hope that the strangers would pass by. After all, they seemed to be just two old people waiting to die!) But Abraham defied human inclinations and hurried out of the tent to intercept the strangers and to offer them extravagant hospitality. As it turned out, they were messengers from God bearing the incredible good news that God had at last set a date for the birth of Sarah's first child: "The stranger said, 'About this time next year I will be sure to come back to you, and Sarah your wife shall have a son' "(Gen 18:10). By making room in his life for mystery, Abraham also made room for happy surprise and incredible promises fulfilled.

This event was not merely an episode in the private history of Abraham; it was a symbol of what it means to live by faith. Saint Paul leaves no doubt on this score. When he looked for an illustration of the faith that he had just described in chapter three of his letter to the Romans, he singled out Abraham who "contemplated his own body, as good as dead (for he was about a hundred years old), and the deadness of Sarah's womb, and never doubted God's promise in unbelief, but, strong in faith, gave honor to God, in the firm conviction of his power to do what he had promised" (Rom 4:19-21). Abraham's human eyes saw nothing but death and defeat, but his eyes of faith saw life and victory . . . and it was his faith, not his reason, that was vindicated! God had turned mysterious for Abraham; he had become a stranger to him. But he persisted in looking for good in the God whose goodness had once been so evident. Thus, by making room for the mystery of God, he made room also for God's ultimate and surprising gift.

In order to emphasize the importance of Abraham's faith as a model for all believers, the biblical author reached into his treasury of ancient lore for a story which would illustrate the sin of unbelief. This is the story of the tower of Babel which, told as it is just before the saga of Abraham, is meant to provide a contrast to Abraham's generosity. Though the tower of Babel is best known as the place where God "made a babble of the language of all the world" (Gen 11:9), it is in fact a tower that was built to defend the people there from the call of God: " 'Come,' they said, 'let us build ourselves a city and a tower with its top in the heavens, and make a name for ourselves; or we shall be dispersed all over the earth' " (Gen 11:4). In the very next chapter, we see how Abraham did not attempt to build a thick wall to protect himself from God's call but instead listened to God's summons and was in effect dispersed over all the earth! The sin of the men of Babel was the sin of those who choose the rational, comprehensible and familiar over the mystery of God's plan. Much later, on the feast of Pentecost, Babel will be reversed as men of many tongues are able to communicate in the Spirit precisely at the moment when they are about to be scattered all over the world to proclaim the good news of Jesus' resurrection.

A New Testament counterpart to the story of Abraham's hospitality to the three strangers is the story of the two men on their way from Jerusalem to Emmaus shortly after the resurrection. They were thoroughly disheartened by what had happened to Jesus. Suddenly, Jesus joined them on the way "but something kept them from seeing who it was" (Luke 24:16). Jesus, their beloved friend, had in fact become a stranger to them. This could happen only because they had expected something from the earthly career of Jesus that was altogether different from what God had planned: ". . . we had been hoping that he was the man to liberate Israel" (Luke 24:21). When the promising career of Jesus ended in ignominious death, they could only conclude that their faith had been betrayed. Thus, the risen Jesus, as stranger, represented the mystery of God's way.

To enter into this divine mystery, the two bewildered men had to put aside old ideas as they listened to Jesus giving them a new interpretation of the Scriptures: "Then he began with Moses and all the prophets, and explained to them the passages which referred to himself in every part of the scriptures" (Luke 24:27). By this time they had reached their home and Jesus was about to leave them. They would have none of that, however; having opened their minds and hearts to him, they opened their home as well: "Stay with us, for evening draws on, and the day is almost over" (Luke 24:29). As they broke the bread of hospitality with him, "their eyes were opened and they recognized him" (Luke 24:31). What they recognized was more than the familiar features of their friend. They were suddenly awakened to a new insight and a new wisdom that attuned them to the mysterious ways of God, for they now saw that the darkest part of the divine mystery — the dying of the Messiah — had become the occasion for the most luminous victory — the Resurrection of Jesus! They had come face to face with the cloud and then, with the guidance of Jesus, the cloud was suddenly transfused with light.

This beautiful story is perfectly at home in the gospel of Luke where Jesus is frequently pictured at table and sometimes even with people who were not considered suitable company for him: ". . . the tax-gatherers and other bad characters were all crowding in to listen to him; and the Pharisees and the doctors of the law began grumbling among themselves: 'This fellow,' they said, 'welcomes sinners and eats with them' "(Luke 15:1-2).

Luke also highlights, in the Acts of the Apostles, the heroic hospitality required of the Jewish-Christian church as she is challenged to accept the Gentiles into the new community of God's people. A Jewish-Christian church making room for the once despised Gentiles is a model for all of us who find it almost impossible to accept some change in our carefully planned lives, whether it is the loss of a dear friend or merely a new way of celebrating the liturgy. Jesus did not eat with disreputable people because he didn't care about their sinfulness but because he saw good in them too and wanted to call it forth. He knew that good and evil are not so simple as we like to imagine. Much that is condemned as evil is simply different or unconventional. Where one is willing, like Jesus, to listen and learn it is often possible to find unsuspected goodness in surprising places. This is an interior journey toward greater sensitivity and awareness; it is another way of finding flowers in the desert.

LUKE: A GOSPEL FOR TRAVELERS

Each of the four evangelists tells the story of Jesus from his own distinctive point of view. In the case of Luke, the public ministry of Jesus is reduced to one great journey from Galilee to Jerusalem. After the stage has been set and the issues have been defined in the Galilean ministry, the signal for the decisive movement toward Jerusalem is given: "As the time approached when he was to be taken up to heaven, he set his face resolutely towards Jerusalem

. . . " (Luke 9:51). To "set one's face" meant to choose a course from which one would never be diverted. It is clear that Jesus went up to Jerusalem more than once but Luke is not primarily interested in history; he wants to present Jesus as a model for the spiritual journey of every human being from the Galilee of self-discovery and self-awareness to the Jerusalem of self-sacrifice before God. For the heart of Jerusalem was the temple; and the heart of the temple was the altar of sacrifice. To understand the message of Jesus, according to Luke, is to make this journey with him.

In all likelihood, Luke was the only biblical author who was not a Jew. Joseph Fitzmyer (*The Gospel of Luke*, I, 42) writes: " . . . I regard Luke as a Gentile Christian, not, however, as a Greek, but as a non-Jewish Semite, a native of Antioch . . . " Since he came from an environment of heartless pagan competition, Luke was especially sensitive to the gracious mercy of God as revealed in the actions and preaching of Jesus. His gospel is the gospel of dramatic pardons. He alone recorded the parable of the prodigal son who was welcomed home with a feast. And he alone recalled the words of Jesus: " . . . I tell you, there will be greater joy in heaven over one sinner who repents than over ninety-nine righteous people who do not need to repent" (Luke 15:7). One wonders if such a daring statement would not have been declared heretical were it not found in the inspired scriptures! For Luke then the whole process of salvation began with the discovery of God's incredible mercy; it all began with "amazing grace." No one is beyond that mercy; no situation is completely hopeless. God does not issue orders from some high throne; he reaches down to lift us from our misery.

The mercy of God gives the freedom and strength to make a faith response. For Luke, this response must be generous, wholehearted and unconditional. God does not play games; if he rescues us, he wants complete loyalty in return: "So also none of you can be a disciple of mine without parting with all his possessions" (Luke 14:33). This does not mean that the follower of Jesus must live in abject poverty. For Luke, affluence and comfort are dangerous because they have a drugging influence which prevents that sensitivity to the needs of others which is essential for the true Christian. The rich man was cast into hell, not simply because he was rich, but because his riches prevented him from seeing Lazarus struggling to survive (Luke 16:19-31). And the rich farmer was condemned, not because he was a successful farmer, but because his full barns became his sole concern in life (Luke 12:16-21). Thus, the journey can be made successfully only if one is detached from worldly goods and truly attached to God and to God's concern for the widow, the orphan and the alien!

MARY, THE PERFECT DISCIPLE

No other book of the Bible speaks more about Mary, the mother of Jesus, than does the gospel of Luke. The Infancy Narratives of Matthew (chapters 1-2) and Luke (chapters 1-2) give us most of our information about Mary and, of the two, Luke's account is far more revealing since Matthew tells the story more from the perspective of Joseph than of Mary. The biblical portrait of Mary is most clearly presented in the scene to which Luke devotes greatest attention, namely, the Annunciation. Mary is here presented as the first generation of Christians had known her, that is, as the humble maiden of Nazareth who willingly embraced the mystery-laden word of God. She was the finest example of the "poor ones" who put God's mysterious will before their own plans (Luke 1:48). Thus, we understand Mary best when we hear her say: "I am the Lord's servant; as you have spoken, so be it" (Luke 1:38).

Because Mary was totally responsive to God's initiative she was chosen to be mother of the divine Messiah. Thus, all her other privileges derive ultimately from her obedience to God's word. This does not imply that she was only passive and demure. On the contrary, it takes great courage to say Yes to God's mysterious call, and more courage still to live out faithfully the implications of that Yes. Furthermore, this courageous response and this fidelity are most authentic when they are as gentle as they are resolute.

When Simeon predicted that Mary would be "pierced to the heart" (Luke 2:35) and when the child Jesus was shown reminding her that he must be about God's business (Luke 2:49), we are given a glimpse of the cost of Mary's fidelity to the word of God in her life. For these were reminders that God would claim her son and would lead him in a way that would be most painful for both of them. Whenever we are asked to suffer by embracing the mystery of life as it is given to us, we should draw consolation from the fact that we are in very good company!

JESUS AND THE SPIRIT IN LUKE'S GOSPEL

In Luke's gospel, the baptism of Jesus was followed almost immediately by his temptation: "Full of the Holy Spirit, Jesus returned from the Jordan, and for forty days was led by the Spirit up and down the wilderness and tempted by the devil" (Luke 4:1-2). It is clear that Jesus is here re-living the experience of Israel in the wilderness of Sinai. This temptation scene is a summary of all the temptations ever experienced by Jesus. As in the case of Israel, he was urged to turn back from the pain and sacrifice of God's way, to reject the mystery for a life that would make sense and be filled with success as humans define it — comfort, recognition, immediate satisfaction. It is significant that Jesus rejected the devil's suggestions each time with a quotation from Deuteronomy. Jesus, unlike many of old Israel, was faithful to the Lord. It is significant also that Jesus was led into the wilderness by the Spirit of God. For it is the Holy Spirit who, as Paul wrote, "explores everything, even the depths of God's own nature" (1 Cor 2:10) and can therefore be a trusted guide on the journey through the uncharted wilderness.

When seen in the larger context of Jesus' public ministry, the temptation was Satan's attempt to deter Jesus from the completion of his journey. He was urged to settle for his early success and popularity. His ministry in Galilee was full of miracles and eloquent speech and enthusiastic response. Why go up to Jerusalem where there was only danger and misunderstanding and uncertainty? But the same Holy Spirit that led Jesus into the wilderness sent him also toward that place of mystery, the only place where faith is really tested and salvation is truly won. In Luke's gospel, Jerusalem is like a magnet: everything else prepares for what must happen there; the names of other towns are generally suppressed to highlight Jerusalem's unique position. It is there, at the center of the mystery, that the ultimate wisdom will be preached on Calvary and the true miracle of resurrection will be witnessed. Only in the dark cloud of mystery and testing did Jesus find the true divine fire.

THE PARACLETE

We are given an insight into how the Spirit helps us to cope with divine mystery in those important passages in John's gospel about the Paraclete. The name "Paraclete" means "one called alongside" and is often found in a juridical context where it can refer to either a prosecuting or defense attorney. Perhaps the best English translation therefore would be "Advocate." For John, then, the Holy Spirit represents the continuing very real, though hidden, presence of God among us now that Jesus, in his physical body, has ascended to heaven. We must remember, of course, that the Spirit is one God with the Father and the Son and is therefore, in a very real sense, their Spirit among us. In fact, Raymond Brown finds it appropriate to say that "the Paraclete is the presence of Jesus when Jesus is absent" (*The Gospel According to John,* Vol II, p.1141).

The Paraclete-Spirit is, according to John, the one who will complete our instruction about the requirements for true discipleship: ". . . your Advocate, the Holy Spirit whom the Father will send in my name, will teach you everything, and will call to mind all that I have told you" (John 14:26). The exact nature of this instruction is made more specific in the following passage:

> When he (the Advocate) comes, he will confute the world, and show where wrong and right and judgment lie. He will convict them of wrong, by their refusal to believe in me; he will convince them that right is on my side, by showing that I go to the Father when I pass from your sight; and he will convince them of divine judgment, by showing that the Prince of this world stands condemned (John 16:8-11).

The Holy Spirit will stand by our side when we find that our Christian convictions put us out of harmony with the views of a secular society and thus expose us to ridicule or hostility. For, working deep within us, the Spirit will show us how wrong the worldly and perhaps popular view is in these crucial areas. Secular society sees sin as anything that disturbs its own conventions or concepts of order; for Christians, however, sin is rejection of the truth taught by Jesus and this truth, which demands that we love and care for all, may very well challenge the violence and injustice that are frequently built into the structure of secular society. It is sinful to defend a system that does not assure economic and political opportunity for all alike. The Spirit will stand with us, Jesus says, when we strive for the ideal of a fair and just society or when we challenge conventions that prevent needed change of any kind.

The Spirit will not only strip away the mask of sin; he will also show that right is on the side of Jesus, that is, that the path traced out by Jesus does not lead to failure and absurdity, as his death seemed to prove, but to victory and fulfillment, as demonstrated by his resurrection. The fact that Jesus goes to the Father when he leaves earth means that his teaching leads to our true homeland and is therefore entirely trustworthy. The resurrection of Jesus has turned everything upside down and has completely changed the meaning of success and failure. True success means henceforth to lead a life of love and service which may indeed appear foolish but which, because it ends in resurrection, is supremely wise. And real failure is to lead a selfish life, seeking and perhaps finding, power and domination, but ending in frustration and terrible disappointment. The Spirit therefore reminds us constantly that the good and right in this life is that only which leads to the Father, where Jesus is enthroned in glory.

Finally, the Spirit instructs us concerning the true meaning of judgment. Satan, the Prince of this world, thought that Jesus was defeated and his teaching discredited when God did not rescue him from the cross. His view is expressed by the chief priests and scribes who showed relief and satisfaction when Jesus was crucified: " 'He saved others,' they said, 'but he cannot save himself. Let the Messiah, the king of Israel, come down now from the cross. If we see that, we shall believe' " (Mark 15:31-32). It seemed at that moment that judgment had been pronounced against Jesus and against everything he stood for. However, the Spirit is present to assure us that that is not the end of the story, that Jesus has risen from the dead, that Satan is the one who stands condemned and that his cynicism is exposed and rejected. Indeed, Satan "is a liar and the father of lies" (John 8:44) for he promotes the false and deceptive doctrine that we are in the world to take care of ourselves, to acquire as much as we can and to hold on to it as long as we can. This doctrine can be very attractive and we may even try to combine it with a veneer of Christian practice but the Spirit speaks to our hearts about the true meaning of Jesus and about the joy reserved for those who dare to follow him.

5
Prophetic Guidance

We have seen that Israel's movement from familiar but fatal Egypt into the life-giving mystery of the wilderness is symbolic of every believer's movement from a familiar but immature past to the testing of mystery in the future as given by God. The same journey from apparent human success to the painful but fruitful embrace of mystery is seen in the career of Jesus as he left friendly Galilee to enter the apparent darkness but true light of Judea and its place of resurrection. This journey represents the essence of all spiritual growth and development. Without it there is only stagnation, frustration and lost opportunities; with it there is pain but also new awareness and ultimately true and lasting freedom. As one might expect, the biblical authors strive in a special way to illuminate and illustrate all the various dimensions of this crucial process. When they do so, they are providing an insight into what is meant by the prophetic phenomenon in the history of Israel and in the life of Jesus.

"I AM WHO I AM" (EXODUS 3:14)

The prophets were Spirit-filled men and women who encouraged and prodded Israel at those critical moments when she was confronting mystery. The essential element in this phase of growth and conversion is aptly summarized in the mysterious divine name that God revealed to Moses when he stood before the burning bush. The *New English Bible* renders this passage: "I am; that is who I am" (Exod 3:14). However, I prefer the traditional and more literal translation: "I am who I am." Most scholars see in this enigmatic name a reference to God's essential mystery and transcendence all the while that he is truly engaged in Israel's history. (See, e.g., Martin Noth, *Exodus,* p. 45).

John Courtney Murray, a Jesuit theologian who is generally recognized as the principal architect of Vatican II's *Declaration on Religious Freedom,* spells out the implications of this divine name. His interpretation is found in the first of a series of lectures given at Yale University and published under the title, *The Problem of God.* What he says there is most helpful in understanding the crucial prophetic phenomenon in the history of Israel and in the life of Jesus.

Murray points out that "I am who I am" is not a very accurate translation of the original Hebrew. In the first place, the Hebrew verb for "I am" is in the imperfect tense which, in Hebrew, always implies unfinished action and therefore would be better translated as "I shall be." Secondly, since the Hebrews always understood "being" in a dynamic and pragmatic rather than a static and theoretical way, the "I am" would be better translated as "I shall be with you." The Hebrews, in other words, were interested in "being" only insofar as it touched them personally. Thus, when the Psalmist says: "The impious fool says in his heart, 'There is no God' " (Ps 14:1), he is not accusing the senseless one of denying the existence of God but only of denying that God cares about his creatures. For, if God does not care, they would reason, he might as well not exist. Hence, the "I am" becomes: I shall be with you, I shall care for you, I shall be your God in an experienced, tangible way. It would mean, therefore, exactly what was intended in the classic covenant formula, "I will become your God and you shall become my people" (Lev 26:12).

This declaration and assurance of effective, caring divine presence seems to be all that needs to be said. But there is a second "I am," separated from the first by the relative pronoun "who."

Murray contends that this "who" introduces a new element which changes significantly the meaning of the second "I am." He spells out the implications of the "who" by translating it "as who I am". "I shall be with you, as who I am, shall I be with you." This expanded translation makes it clear that the "who" introduces the decisive element of God's freedom and sovereignty, that is, of the essential divine mystery. God promises to be with his people truly and effectively but not in a way that will compromise his essential uniqueness, holiness, freedom and mystery. In other words, God remains God even as he truly condescends to our condition.

With this in mind, the second "I am" takes on new meaning. Having corrected any possible misunderstanding of his presence to Israel, God reasserts his true presence in a way that respects his sovereignty and mystery but is totally loving, caring and effective. As Murray puts it:

> The text, thus understood, contains a threefold revelation — of God's immanence in history, of his transcendence to history, and of his transparence through history. God first asserts the fact of his presence in the history of his people: 'I shall be there.' Second, he asserts the mystery of his own being: 'I shall be there as who I am.' Third, he asserts that, despite his absence in mystery, he will make himself known to his people: 'As who I am shall I be there' (*The Problem of God*, p. 10).

God's "immanence in history" is manifested when he is present in humanly comprehensible ways, in ways that meet our expectations of divine goodness and assistance. Thus, God was present to Israel when he gave freedom to the slaves in Egypt or victory and empire to David. And he was present in this way to the people of Galilee when Jesus healed their sick and drove out demons. This is a good and necessary presence for we could never be free enough to deal with God's mystery if we were not strengthened by such obvious blessings as good parents, educational opportunities, special talents, friends, good health and the like. But God will not leave us in this childrens' paradise which is so much less than his love wishes for us.

God's "transcendence to history" is manifested when he is no longer present in the ways that we understand and appreciate; indeed, he seems suddenly to be absent. This apparent absence of God was experienced by Israel when the empire of David collapsed and was followed by foreign conquest and oppression. Israel suffered under the Assyrians and then the Babylonians as the powerful God of the Exodus seemed to lose interest in them and to abandon them to their tragic fate. And, in the ministry of Jesus, the halcyon days of Galilee disappeared and were replaced with the dark clouds of misunderstanding, rejection and hostility. At the darkest moment, Jesus cries out with the Psalmist, "My God, my God, why hast thou forsaken me?" (Mark 15:34 and Ps 22:1). God transcends history at those times when he no longer conforms to our human understanding of what divine goodness should mean. He asserts his freedom and uniqueness and sovereignty; he becomes mysterious, apparently absent.

This is the prophetic moment. The prophets appear then and bear witness to the continued goodness and concern of God for us, in spite of contrary appearances. They cannot dispel the mystery but they can be good counsellors who help us to cope with the mystery by assuring us that God is now asking us to live in trust, to believe that faithfulness and perseverance will lead to a much better presence. Thus, the prophets are messengers of hope; they bear witness to the gift in the mystery, to the fire in the cloud.

Finally, God is "transparent through history" because his true and most gracious presence will be on his terms. God has not really left the scene but he has changed the manner of his presence. He is actually more present and more loving now than ever because he is now present as he always intended to be, in his own preferred way. It is we who must change, be converted, be opened up to receive and entertain the new, better presence of the Lord. When we give up old, childish ways, when we listen to and trust the prophets, then we truly meet the Lord, and history becomes transparent as God is seen everywhere. This is the beginning of the Kingdom of God and those who discover it would never want to return to David's kingdom or even to the happy but somewhat unreal days of Galilee.

Thus, the mysterious divine name can summarize what the Bible means by conversion, growth, journeying. This movement from presence on our terms, through apparent absence, to presence on God's terms is so all-pervasive in the Scriptures that it could be called the "genetic code" of the Bible, by which all biblical realities are identified. This also shows how important trust is in our relations with God. If we do not truly come to know the Lord in his goodness and mercy, we will not be able to trust him when we must enter the time of darkness and apparent absence. Then, like Israel in the wilderness, we will want to return to the familiar but fatal time of our immaturity. But if we can live in trust and struggle through the time of darkness we will emerge into a new world of far better and more real presence and awareness.

The relationship of children to their parents often provides on a human level an illustration of this challenge to trust a former experience of love at a time of trial. I recall how my niece, Clare Ann, had begun her first year at school with great enthusiasm. By the third day, however, she had had enough and locked herself in the bathroom shortly before the school bus was to arrive. Her mother pleaded with her to come out, reminding her of the importance of making a good first impression at school. Finally, she did come out and, as she snatched her book bag and went out the door, she said over her shoulder in a loud voice, "Now, what about all that love and stuff?!" She did what she did not want to do because she knew that her mother really did love her but she needed to protest that this love was becoming too mysterious, too challenging. At that moment, when the benefits of education were not apparent to her, she complied because she had experienced love and trusted its demands even though that love now caused pain. When she graduated from school, she understood and was grateful for a love that demanded trust and risked giving pain for a greater good. Heaven will give the same proof to those who trust the Lord's goodness.

Saint Teresa of Avila spelled out the implications of this in our relationship with God when she said one day to the Lord: "No wonder you have so few friends, considering how badly you treat them!" When things do not go as planned, when illness strikes us or a loved one, when a tragic accident occurs, we wonder about the love of God who would permit this to happen when we have tried to be faithful to him. We sometimes hear people say: "It seems so unfair that some very old and suffering people, who want to die, cannot do so while my loved one is dying while still very young and in spite of all my prayers." This is the critical prophetic moment when God turns mysterious and we struggle in the darkness. The prophets in our lives will not try to explain the mystery but will simply bear witness to God's continued love, now more real than ever, as they assure us that this painful experience will open us to a far greater gift of God than we have ever known before. We must continue to praise and thank the Lord for a love that is very real and tender, even if it is now hidden.

ELIJAH, FRIEND OF MYSTERY

The glory of David's empire represents symbolically what God can do, on a merely human and political level, to demonstrate his love and good will toward his chosen people. But it was not meant to last. When King Solomon replaced his father on the throne of Israel, it marked the end of an era. For Solomon lost the momentum that David had provided; he became conservative, defensive and oppressive. As Walter Brueggemann has pointed out, his reign was characterized by "incredible well-being and affluence," by "oppressive social policy," expressed in the form of forced labor, and by the "establishment of a controlled, static religion" (*The Prophetic Imagination*, pp. 32-34). Thus, Solomon was able in a few short years to neutralize and even negate the idealism of the Exodus. Even the temple built by Solomon was an ambiguous symbol, for it emphasized the static and established nature of his religion as opposed to the tent which had been, until then, the habitation of God with his journeying people. Under Solomon, religion became massive and monumental, protective of elite privileges, unsuited for the journey of faith.

This betrayal of the Exodus continued in varying degrees during the time of the divided kingdom. It reached a climax, however, when Ahab sat on the throne of the northern kingdom of Israel, with Jezebel at his side (869-850 BCE). The prophet Elijah then appeared and his confrontation with King Ahab illuminated both the extent of Israel's apostasy and the nature of prophetic witness.

Ahab sat on the throne and wore the crown but he no longer represented the soul of Israel. He was dominated by the imperious Jezebel, a Phoenician woman, who symbolized both the enticement and the destructive influence of pagan religion. The true Israel was committed to care of the orphan, the widow and the alien, but when wealthy Ahab coveted the little vineyard of Naboth, he permitted Jezebel to arrange its acquisition by deceit and violence. Then Jezebel turned the vineyard over to her whimpering husband with the words: "Get up and take possession of the vineyard which Naboth refused to sell you, for he is no longer alive" (1 Kgs 21:15). When Ahab accepted this without a qualm it was clear that Israel's ideals had been irreparably compromised.

But those ideals were still alive in the wilderness of Tishbe, beyond the Jordan, where the prophet Elijah lived. The stories about him are vivid and dramatic and the biblical author obviously delights in recounting them. They show him raising a poor widow's son from the dead, winning a dramatic contest with Jezebel's pagan prophets on Mount Carmel and then fleeing from Jezebel to Mount Horeb where he heard the voice of the Lord, not in the wind or earthquake or fire, but in the "low murmuring sound""of God's gentle power (1 Kgs 19:12). In all these stories, Elijah is portrayed as God's man, as one who exercises life-giving power, confronts evil without fear and then struggles with the mystery of God in his own life. He dwelt in the wilderness because he represented God's mystery, freedom and sovereignty. He was a will-o'-the-wisp who could not be pinned down to any fixed abode

(1 Kgs 18:7-16) because God's mystery is not to be controlled, not even by the king.

Because he was a friend of divine mystery, Elijah became the model of what a prophet should be. He was, in a very real sense, the prophets' prophet. As a wilderness man, he set himself against that human order and control represented by King Ahab and, beyond him, by the Egyptian Pharaoh. He, like all the prophets, strove mightily to restore Israel's religious consciousness — her sensitivity for God's presence and her devotion to the Exodus ideals. His task was difficult and rarely popular for most people like what is clear and understandable here and now while he stood for a mystery that would make sense only at the end. He, like all the prophets, pleaded with and threatened Israel by turns, urging her to enter the darkness, to take the narrow road of loving responsibility, to trust the Lord in every circumstance.

The role of the prophet in every age will be difficult but very rewarding. One can scarcely imagine a more exquisite form of charity than the loving and firm support given to one who is challenged to move ahead yet tempted to go back. This is true whether it is simply a matter of choosing the mature, decent decision or of coping with some tragic event or of accepting old age and death from the God of mystery and love. If a reward is promised to one who gives a glass of water (Mk 9:41), how much greater will be the reward of the prophet, who gives hope and life, even as he struggles with mystery himself!

Elijah did not write a book and is therefore not as well known as Isaiah or Jeremiah or Ezechiel. But he did what every prophet must do: he lived the mystery to which he bore witness. For the prophet too must struggle in faith and when he declares God's goodness wrapped in mystery he is simply witnessing to what he himself has discovered. After his great victory on Mount Carmel, Elijah felt abandoned and fled from the wrath of Jezebel. But when he heard God's soft voice at Mount Horeb, he knew that there was fire in that cloud, that God is present in weakness even more readily than in strength.

Part of the prophet's pain comes from the fact that, after sowing hope in a field of doubt, he is often not permitted to see the harvest. Thus, Elijah was called by God unexpectedly and had to pass his mantle to Elisha. As Raymond Brown has pointed out, this is a common theme in the Bible: Moses turned his unfinished task over to Joshua and the teaching of Jesus is completed by the Paraclete (*The Gospel According to John,* Vol II, p. 1138). We are frequently tempted to pull back from initiating a project because we fear that we will not live to see it completed. Why plant a tree whose fruit you will never enjoy? But the one who understands that we are always partners with God in whatever we do, will not hesitate to make the best contribution he can and gladly leave the rest to God or to others under God.

Moses, Elijah and Jesus represent the entire Bible; surely what is true of them must be an ideal for all of us! There is something profoundly selfless about enthusiastic support by older people for the beginnings of long-term projects. This is also true of good teachers who are perfectly willing to turn their best students over to the care and appreciation of others; or of good parents who urge their children to leave the security of home for the challenge of their own careers. Prophetic love is always painful but it is also wonderfully fruitful.

JESUS AND THE TEMPLE

The prophetic role of Jesus is seen clearly in his attitude toward the temple. When he was arrested and brought to trial before the Jewish religious court (called the Sanhedrin), the primary charge brought against him was an accusation of disrespect for the temple. "Finally two men alleged that he had said, 'I can pull down the temple of God, and rebuild it in three days' " (Matt 26:60-61). The charge is disputed and inconclusive (see Mark 14:59), but there is little doubt that what the Jewish authorities found most objectionable in the activity of Jesus had something to do with his challenge, not only to the temple, but to what the temple represented.

We have already emphasized the importance of the journey for Israel's religious consciousness and we have noted that this made the temple an ambiguous symbol since it tended to represent a static, established concept of religion. Most of the prophets were nervous about the temple and about its meaning for the people. Jeremiah spoke most clearly about this, warning the people not to put a blind trust in the temple, as if God were somehow identified with it and would have to defend it at all cost: "You keep saying, 'This place is the temple of the Lord, the temple of the Lord, the temple of the Lord!' This catchword of yours is a lie; put no trust in it" (Jer 7:4). The image of the tent was far more appropriate for describing the nature of God's presence with his people. He travelled with his people; he did not sit in a shrine like the pagan deities. This does not mean that the temple (or any monumental church) is in itself dangerous; but it does point up the need to avoid some aspects of its symbolic message.

When Jesus was accused of speaking disrespectfully of the temple, it can be assumed that this charge was based, at least in part, upon that profoundly prophetic action by which he cleansed the temple of the money-changers. This episode is recorded in all the gospels, although the Synoptics are probably correct in placing it near the end of Jesus' public ministry; indeed it may have been the proverbial last straw as far as the religious authorities were concerned.

> So they came to Jerusalem, and he went into the temple and began driving out those who bought and sold in the temple. He upset the tables of the money-changers and the seats of the dealers in pigeons; and he would not allow anyone to use the temple court as a thoroughfare for carrying goods. Then he began to teach them, and said, "Does not Scripture say, 'My house shall be called a house of prayer for all the nations'? But you have made it a robbers' cave." The chief priests and the doctors of the law heard of this and sought some means of making away with him . . . (Mark 11:15-18).

It is clear that Jesus is protesting a profanation of the temple but it is not so easy to see just what this abuse might have been. The selling of animals for sacrifice and the changing of money for the temple tax (which could be paid only in imageless coins) were a necessary service, not an abuse. This practice could have become objectionable if it were done in the temple precincts, instead of at a respectful distance, or if it involved exorbitant prices. In any case, the atmosphere was noisy, commercial and competitive; it was not conducive to prayer or recollection. There were earlier prophetic complaints about such abuses, as in the text from Jeremiah (7:11) referred to in Mark's version (above). The cleansing of the temple was seen therefore as one of the Messianic blessings: "So when that time comes, no trader shall again be seen in the house of the Lord of Hosts" (Zechariah 14:21).

The cleansing of the temple by Jesus was certainly much more than just the correction of a liturgical abuse. It was a prophetic gesture and a signal of the arrival of the Messianic age when the worship of God would be purified and made truly worthy. Jesus is therefore protesting against what the religion of his day had become; instead of a saving and liberating power, it had been turned into a rigid, suffocating system of human prescriptions for the purpose of protecting and preserving ecclesiastical power. Jesus complained frequently about the distortion of the original meaning of the Torah: "You have made God's law null and void out of respect for your tradition" (Matt 15:6). Since the temple symbolized God's presence in Israel, the very meaning of that presence was compromised by the use of that temple to support ecclesiastical power and privilege. When Jesus drove the money-changers out of the temple he was attacking the very center of that abusive power and thus was asserting a sharp distinction between that power and the true meaning of God's presence. I like to think that Jesus took swipes at the pillars of the temple and not just at the tables of the money-changers! The chief priests and scribes understood immediately that he was challenging their authority and condemning their use of power. Hence, their consternation and their conclusion that he had become intolerable — a decision that led directly to the Passion climax.

It is the role of the prophet in every age to resist the tendency of religion to become so institutionalized that it no longer leaves any room for the creative Spirit. Since religion has strong social implications, it must develop some structure in order to be efficient and effective in its work. However, a balance must be maintained between formal structure and personal creativity. The roles of king and prophet must both be safeguarded. And, of the two, it is the role of the prophet that is most often sacrificed, simply because it is easier to defend the logic of order than the devotion to divine mystery. But divine mystery is far more likely than any order to bring true responsibility and ultimate salvation.

The "temple mentality," which emphasizes institutional structure and order, is not necessarily the attitude of wicked people. Most often it will be espoused by sincere and well-meaning persons who simply succumb to the very attractive temptation to preserve what one understands rather than to take the risk of making changes or even of encouraging more imaginative approaches to problems. Walter Brueggemann, in his book *The Prophetic Imagination,* has succeeded admirably in sketching the implications of this polarity. He points out that true prophecy not only challenges the old, entrenched order by providing a sharp critique of its Pharaonic, secularizing tendencies but also provides a new vision or "alternative consciousness" (p. 13) which releases the creative power of the Spirit in God's people.

In this way, the prophets strove to restore the dynamism of the Exodus which was lost under Solomon and other kings, notably Ahab. One will note also that it was precisely this imaginative initiative that permitted David to defeat Goliath while Saul was immobilized by his inability to break with tradition! It was this creative spirit also that guided Jesus as he condemned rigid, outmoded structures and prescriptions, proclaiming instead that the true role of religion is to liberate for responsibility.

THE PROPHETIC MOMENT OF
JESUS' TRANSFIGURATION

In the gospel of Mark, the transfiguration is situated at the center of the public ministry. It is preceded by the ministry in Galilee and followed by the ministry in Judea and especially in Jerusalem. Thus, it represents a major landmark on that road that took Jesus from the successes and popularity of Galilee to passion and death in Judea. As Arthur Michael Ramsey puts it: "Thus the Transfiguration seems to stand at a watershed in the ministry of Jesus, and to be a height from which the reader looks down on one side upon the Galilean ministry and on the other side upon the Via Crucis" (*The Glory of God and the Transfiguration of Christ*, p. 101). Its location in the gospel is such an important consideration that Mark introduces it, contrary to his usual practice, with a chronological reference: "Six days later . . ."(Mark 9:2). In this way, he alerts us to the importance of an event that occurred just before and which helps us to understand the meaning of the transfiguration of Jesus.

What had happened just six days earlier was the questioning of the disciples by Jesus at Caesarea Philippi and the first prediction of the passion. Both of these happenings are of great importance, the first because it signaled the end of a phase in the instruction of the disciples and the second because it introduced the new and surprising message that would constitute their final instruction by the Master. The questioning of the disciples is not unlike an academic examination at the end of a phase of schooling; the questions are concerned with the primary and fundamental matter of his role or mission: "On the way he asked his disciples, 'Who do men say I am?' They answered, 'Some say John the Baptist, others Elijah, others one of the prophets.' 'And you,' he asked, 'who do you say I am?' Peter replied, 'You are the Messiah'" (Mark 8:27-29). Peter's answer was the right one. The miracles of Jesus were indeed intended to establish him clearly as God's Messiah, as the promised and long awaited savior of Israel. But this was still a revelation on human terms and according to human expectations. We are still with the first "I am" of the mysterious name: "I am who I am." For, as will soon appear, Peter is thinking of a political, this-worldly Messiah.

The mystery of the Messianic mission as God understands it emerges in the following verses: " . . . and he began to teach them that the Son of man had to undergo great sufferings. . . He spoke about it plainly" (Mark 8:31-32). This is the first clear indication that the ministry of Jesus would lead him to suffering and death, rather than to political triumph over the Roman occupation army. It is the revelation of God's freedom, sovereignty and mystery. For God's plan is not at all what the disciples had expected. In fact, they were stunned by this announcement. Peter took Jesus aside and asked him to tell them that he did not really mean what he had said. But Jesus insisted, telling Peter that to oppose him on this point would be equivalent to joining the forces of Satan, God's perennial adversary.

So there it was: the terrible mystery of a Messiah who is abandoned to suffering and death! The disciples had indeed arrived at the "graduate" level of their education! It was in this context where divine sovereignty had intercepted and cancelled human plans that the surprising event of transfiguration took place.

The transfiguration story is made up of both historical and theological elements. There is no good reason to doubt that this event did occur, although the name of the mountain where it happened is not given and Mount Tabor is only an educated guess. It is doubtful that Moses and Elijah could have been photographed there; they were there solely for the purpose of emphasizing the significance of this event. It is as if Moses and Elijah, representing the Law and the Prophets, were saying: What is happening here is what we were teaching in the entire Old Testament! They are there also because they too had a "mountain experience" — Moses on Mount Sinai, where he received the Ten Commandments, and Elijah on Mount Carmel, when he defeated the prophets of Baal. Thus, encountering God on a mountain top was already the traditional way to discover God's secret purposes in a profoundly mystical experience.

The presence of Moses and Elijah thus helps us to answer the most important question about the transfiguration: What was the nature of the mysterious illumination of Jesus, so that "his clothes became dazzling white, with a whiteness no bleach on earth could equal" (Mark (9:3)? It has been customary to see this as an illumination that came from heaven for the encouragement of the disciples who had just been saddened by the prediction of the passion. This interpretation, however, seems highly unlikely. For one thing, the reaction of Peter was not one of relief at seeing that Jesus was still affirmed by God. Rather, as Mark tells us, "he did not know what to say; they were so terrified" (9:6). Peter realized that he was in the presence of God and suggested building three tents (9:5) but that seemed to be merely an awkward way of responding to divine mystery. The impetuous Peter must always respond in some way, even when it is inappropriate!

The true meaning of the transfiguration involves Jesus far more than the disciples. It is an interior, spiritual experience with external and bodily effects. The aura of light that surrounded Jesus was the result of a profound discovery or new awareness on his part. It was as if something obscure and meaningless had suddenly become evident and wonderfully meaningful. What was this profound, mystical discovery on the part of Jesus? It was the awareness that God would bring Messianic salvation, not in the human way of power and miracles but in the divine way of love and sacrifice. The transfiguration then would mark a turning-point in Jesus' own consciousness of his mission and would be a profound mystical discovery of the wonderful wisdom of God who turns the unpromising vulnerability of loving into stunning and lasting victory.

The illumination of Jesus is followed by a message from heaven: "Then a cloud appeared, casting its shadow over them, and out of the cloud came a voice: 'This is my Son, my Beloved; listen to him'" (Mark 9:7). These words are very similar to those spoken at Jesus' baptism (Mark 1:11), except that here they are spoken about him rather than to him, and here the admonition is added to "listen to him." The strong affirmation of the Son by his heavenly

Father is given for the benefit of all who might find it hard to believe that a sacrificial death would be the chosen means of divine salvation. It is a powerful and unqualified declaration of God's commitment to the suffering Messiah. The words, "Listen to him," are addressed to the disciples and, beyond them, to all his followers. It is as if God were saying that it is precisely now, when Jesus begins his journey of loving sacrifice, that he becomes a teacher of divine wisdom. Everything prior to this has been merely a preparation; it is in loving sacrifice that God's message through Jesus is truly given.

THE TRANSFIGURATION AND CHRISTIANS

As long as the transfiguration is considered to be something that happened only to Jesus, we will never understand its real meaning. Once again, the gospels are not interested in the private history of Jesus; they show us a Jesus who led the way for us and whom we must follow on that way. When we realize that for Jesus the transfiguration was a sign of his deeper understanding of what his mission really involved, we will be ready to see that every follower of Jesus must go through a similar experience on the journey of faith and continuous conversion.

The typical Christian will recognize a "Galilean" period in life when he or she was young and strong, discovering new worlds, earning degrees, winning battles, driving out the demons of fear and low self-esteem, working the "miracles" of begetting children and buying or building a house. During this time there is, despite occasional setbacks, a feeling of expanding horizons and growing confidence.

Somewhat later, as middle age sets in, there are small but unmistakable hints of the fragility and finality of this world. One senses the onset of physical and mental decline and knows that it can only grow worse as time passes. Retirement is often a traumatic experience as one interrupts the rhythm of a lifetime of regular work and is left with too much time to think about the unpromising future. Though we know that this will happen and make plans for it with insurance and payment into pension plans, it remains the unknown and generally unwanted land of a threatening future. This is, in a very real sense, the mystery of the wilderness. Here we can truly walk with ancient Israel as we are tempted to live in a reverie about the nostalgic past while fearing the fierce "giants" who loom ahead of us. We can also walk with Jesus as he becomes ever more aware of the pain and suffering that await him in Judea.

It is at this critical moment in our lives that we encounter the reality of divine mystery. Frequently, our prayers are least comforting precisely when our need of support seems greatest. The past is gone, the future is bleak and God is silent. We are sorely tempted to make some kind of accommodation by developing a tough but costly sense of "realism" that is almost cynical. Was it not foolish to have entertained such hopes and expectations? Perhaps the crepe-hangers were more prophetic than we thought. As we try to make adjustments, we feel a twinge of disappointment, perhaps even of resentment, as we wonder why God should have given such capacity for hope to fragile humans like ourselves.

From the perspective of Christian faith, however, this is the great opportunity of our lives. In this wilderness or desert experience, we can in one day make more progress toward what God wants us to be than we could in a whole year in the lush valleys of our youth. In those salad years we were receiving the affirmation that would give us the freedom and strength to make the most of this great opportunity for growth and maturing. It is as if we were waiting all those early years just for this chance to sing in the rain, to prove our trust in the reality and goodness of God! And it keeps getting better as time goes on. As the rational and secular side of us settles into an old age of resignation to weakness and defeat, the believing side sees that growing old provides ever more opportunities for love, concern, prayer and sacrifice. The days of building monuments are over but faith reminds us that life was never meant for that anyway. Those "miracles" of Galilee were simply a prelude to the time of patient loyalty and final self-giving that will prepare for God's great miracle of resurrection!

This is the time of the prophets. They give assurance of God's continued love and fidelity, in spite of appearances. They help us to stop looking back toward the "good old days" that are past and to fix our gaze instead on the horizon of the future, bright with God's promises of a land of milk and honey for those who refuse to succumb to the siren song of self-pity and despair. They remind us too that it is only by reaching out in concern for others that the declining years can become the best years of our lives. They counsel us to invest more and more of our time in nourishing the immortal spirit of love rather than in the hopeless task of preserving a mortal body. Saint Paul speaks of this when he writes to the Corinthians: "Wherever we go we carry death with us in our body, the death that Jesus died, that in this body also life may reveal itself, the life that Jesus lives . . . No wonder we do not lose heart! Though our outward humanity is in decay, yet day by day we are inwardly renewed" (2 Cor 4:10, 16).

This is also the time when we can ourselves become prophetic witnesses. God has so arranged matters that the assurance which we cannot give to ourselves we can give effectively to others. And so, by providing consolation and courage for others, we cast bread on the waters (Ecclesiastes 11:1), as we await with confidence the comfort and encouragement that we too will surely need. Those who have grown old are especially qualified to provide this exquisite prophetic service, for they can speak from lived experience. They have been there, and so their advice has a special cogency and power. What a contrast there is between an old age of bitterness and complaints that make others fear to grow old and an old age of love, concern and wise advice that fills others with admiration and gratitude!

It may be very difficult at first to search for divine gift and promise in a future that has become dark with threat, but there is a tremendous power in the magnetism of God's future. Once one manages to turn his face toward that sun, the petals will unfold and the darkness will be dispelled. Saint Benedict speaks of this in the Prologue of his *Rule* for monks:

> Do not be daunted immediately by fear and run away from the road that leads to salvation. It is bound to be narrow at the outset. But as we progress in this way of life and in faith, we shall run on the path of God's commandments, our hearts overflowing with the inexpressible delight of love (*RB 1980, Prologue*, 48-49).

This is also illustrated by the universally appealing picture of a small child learning to walk. At the proper moment, the child is sent across the room from one parent to another. As it begins this hazardous journey it looks back to the nearest parent for encouragment but, at a critical moment near the middle of the journey, it looks ahead to the other parent, puts out its hands and hurries into welcoming arms. We too tend at first to look back at our accomplishments to give meaning to our lives but, if we follow the lead of faith and grace, we will eventually dare to look ahead and to run expectantly toward the welcoming arms of our Father in heaven!

6

Living in Hope

The nature of every journey is determined by its goal or destination. If the goal is Jerusalem or Rome or some famous shrine like Lourdes, it is called a pilgrimage. The goal may not be a place at all but simply enjoyment or relaxation and then it is called a cruise or a tourist jaunt. Sometimes the journey is a search for some reality which is perceived to be essential in order to make sense out of life: thus, some have searched for Shangri-La or for the Holy Grail. This kind of journey would be closest to the biblical search for the Promised Land. In all these journeys, the goal and its desirability will determine how much hardship one is willing to accept on the journey. People are usually more willing to accept hardships in order to make a pilgrimage than for the pleasures of sight-seeing; and the searchers for the Holy Grail will endure any hardship and persevere at all cost. This yearning for the goal which gives meaning and purpose to the journey is called hope.

HOPE: MANNA IN THE WILDERNESS

After the Israelites had escaped from the bondage of Egypt, they wandered for forty years in the Sinai wilderness before taking a circuitous route through Edom and Moab to reach Canaan, the Promised Land, from the east. They took this long route because they did not think they could enter Canaan from the south after hearing from their scouts of the "giants" who occupied that land. While in the wilderness of Sinai, the Israelites were nourished in part by a mysterious food called "manna." The provision of this food is described in Exodus:

> The Israelites complained to Moses and Aaron in the wilderness and said, 'If only we had died at the Lord's hand in Egypt, where we sat round the flesh-pots and had plenty of bread to eat! But you have brought us out into this wilderness to let this whole assembly starve to death!'
>
> The Lord said to Moses, 'I will rain down bread from heaven for you. Each day the people shall go out and gather a day's supply, so that I can put them to the test and see whether they will follow my instructions or not' (16:2-4).

One should note that the favorable description of conditions in Egypt is simply a case of convenient memory; the past is easily glamorized from a safe distance!

The nature of this "bread from heaven" is described in more detail in the book of Numbers:

> The manna looked like coriander seed, the color of gum resin. The people went about collecting it, ground it up in hand-mills or pounded it in mortars, then boiled it in the pot and made it into cakes. It tasted like butter-cakes. When dew fell on the camp at night, the manna fell with it (11:7-9).

Although the biblical account suggests a miraculous origin for the manna, it is believed to be the droplets of sap secreted from the tamarisk tree and hardened in the cool temperature of the night. It can then be gathered in the morning and is edible. In the tradition of Israel, however, this manna acquired a profound symbolic meaning: it is the spiritual nourishment provided by God to sustain those who are making the journey of faith. Thus, biblical faith and hope are inseparable, for faith responds to the call to journey and hope provides motivation as it yearns for the fulfillment at the end of the journey.

This close relationship of faith and hope is reflected in a celebrated description of faith in the letter to the Hebrews: "And what is faith? Faith gives substance to our hopes, and makes us certain of realities we do not see" (11:1). The Greek original clearly indicates that faith "gives substance to our hopes" by providing a basis or an undergirding for hoping. Faith enables us to discover the goodness of God experientially and this discovery causes us then to yearn for the full experience of that goodness at the end of time, at the end of the journey, in the Promised Land beyond the wilderness. This final experience of love, peace and harmony for which we, in our brokenness and incompleteness, yearn ever more strongly belongs to the "realities we do not see." Faith convinces us that these spiritual realities are, like God, more real than anything we can touch or see. By hope we yearn for them and for the God who is at their center and thus we are nourished as we move forward on the journey. This spiritual manna is so important and so necessary because the journey is through the wilderness, that is, it is a journey that renounces the immediate and tantalizing food of selfish satisfaction and can therefore be painful and arduous.

The importance of the manna of hope for Christian living was brought home to me in an experience of my early years — an experience that almost all can recognize in some event of their own lives. I was not quite thirteen years old when I went off to a boarding high school for boys. I had grown up in a large family on a small farm in the Allegheny mountains and I was desperately homesick during that first year. When I finally went home for Christmas vacation, I remember the train ride from Latrobe to Cresson. It was not at all a scenic ride; there were mining towns with heaps of slag and the miles of Bethlehem steel mills before pollution control. But the piles of dirty slag seemed like mounds of jewels and this bleak winter landscape seemed more beautiful than the valley of the Engadin in the Swiss Alps — because I was going home! I would soon see my family and friends . . . and the new calf! The expectation of homecoming thus transformed my journey experience. In a similar way, we can have our difficult journey through life illuminated and transfigured by the hope that anticipates our arrival at our true and perfect home.

THE MANNA OF EUCHARIST: JOHN 6

The fullest Christian development of the manna symbolism is found in chapter 6 of the gospel of John. There the manna is reinterpreted by Jesus to signify, first of all, his life-giving teaching, and then, his own body and blood. It is important to realize, as Raymond Brown points out (*The Gospel According to John*, Vol. 1, pp. 272-74), that the eucharistic interpretation of the "bread of life" is found only in a relatively short section of this lengthy discourse, namely, in 6:51-58. This relatively brief treatment, far from minimizing the importance of the eucharist, actually enhances it by giving it a very careful and significant introduction. It is like a jewel displayed to full advantage by a perfect set.

Chapter 6 begins with two miracle stories which establish a context for the bread of life discourse. The first of these (6:1-15) is John's version of the miraculous multiplication of loaves and fishes. The fact that this is the only miracle of Jesus' public ministry that is found in all four gospels attests to its importance for the early Christian communities. All versions of the story are meant to underline for Christians the importance of making the most of limited resources. Although the action of Jesus does illustrate his special power, the story is not told simply to cause us to stand in admiration of that power. Rather, it is a story that shows how Jesus dealt with a basic human problem. First, there was the large crowd in need of food; then, the disciples declared their inability to cope with the problem: "There is a boy here who has five barley loaves and two fishes; but what is that among so many?" (6:9); finally, Jesus simply took the loaves and fishes and distributed them: "Then Jesus took the loaves, gave thanks, and distributed them to the people as they sat there. He did the same with the fishes, and they had as much as they wanted" (6:11).

What Jesus did was to set an example for his followers. They will be faced with many problems which, humanly speaking, will appear insuperable. They must then draw from their resources of nature and faith and simply do what they can, trusting that God will provide what is still lacking. The fact that there are twelve baskets of fragments left after all have had their fill is presented as proof that God's help will not fail those who in faith make the most of their limited resources instead of succumbing to the paralyzing influence of despair. John's version of the story differs from the others by noting that the bread available was the coarse and plain barley bread of the poor and that, after the multiplication, all the remnants must be collected "so that nothing may be lost" (6:12). In this way, he prepares for his later comments on the eucharistic bread of life which represents a transformation of common bread into the precious Body of Jesus.

The second introductory story recounts an episode in which Jesus walks on the water (6:16-21). The disciples are shown in a boat buffeted by a storm: "By now a strong wind was blowing and the sea grew rough" (6:18). Suddenly and unexpectedly, "they saw Jesus walking on the sea and approaching the boat. They were terrified, but he called out, 'It is I; do not be afraid.' Then they were ready to take him aboard, and immediately the boat reached the land they were making for" (6:19-21). This story is full of Exodus motifs: the scene of the disciples tossed by a turbulent sea is reminiscent of the chaotic condition of Israel in slavery; the appearance of Jesus walking on the waters recalls Israel's passing miraculously through the waters and Jesus announces his presence with the words "It is I" (6:20) (literally, "I am"), which recalls the name of the God of Exodus (Exod 3:14). The arrival safely at the shore represents the salvation that God gave to those rescued from chaos. This story is especially appropriate as a preparation for the bread of life discourse because it reminds us of God's life-giving power and provides a setting for the Exodus story of the manna which becomes the immediate occasion for Jesus' words about the new bread from heaven.

Some of those who had witnessed the multiplication of loaves and fishes later found Jesus who told them that they must go beyond their hunger for ordinary food: "You must work, not for this perishable food, but for the food that lasts, the food of eternal life" (6:27). They asked him what they should do to find this nourishment, and he said: "believe in the one whom he (God) has sent" (6:29).

> They said, 'What sign can you give us to see, so that we may believe you? . . . Our ancestors had manna to eat in the desert; as Scripture says, "He gave them bread from heaven to eat." Jesus answered, 'I tell you this; the truth is, not that Moses gave you the bread from heaven, but that my Father gives you the real bread from heaven. The bread that God gives comes down from heaven and brings life to the world . . . I am the bread of life' (6:30-35).

In this passage, Jesus clearly states that the new and better nourishment comes through belief in him. This food far surpasses that offered by Moses in the wilderness of Sinai. It is better because it is a nourishment that results in eternal life: "I am the bread of life. Your forefathers ate the manna in the desert and they are dead. I am speaking of the bread that comes down from heaven, which a man may eat, and never die" (6:48-50). It is by faith in Jesus that this life-giving nourishment is received, as Jesus states most emphatically: "In truth, in very truth I tell you, the believer possesses eternal life" (6:47).

In this segment of the bread of life discourse, therefore, Jesus identifies the new bread from heaven, not yet as his body and blood, but as his teaching. To embrace this teaching means to accept and live by his words; it means to turn away from selfish behavior and to begin to love and serve and care for others; in a word, it means to become like Jesus. As Raymond Brown has pointed out (*The Gospel According to John*, Vol.1, p.275), there is a clear biblical precedent for the description of teaching or revelation under the imagery of bread and wine. Thus, in Proverbs, Lady Wisdom invites all to partake of her riches with the words, "Come, dine with me and taste the wine that I have spiced" (9:5). Isaiah likewise compares God's life-giving word to the rain that comes down from heaven and causes the earth to "blossom and bear fruit, and give seed for sowing and bread to eat" (55:10). This bread and wine of true teaching gives a nourishment that produces eternal life because the unselfish path of Jesus leads to true and lasting life, whereas all other paths lead to frustration and death. It is a difficult teaching because it cuts across natural tendencies but it is the only nourishment that can keep the believer moving ahead in the journey to the Promised Land.

After Jesus had identified the new manna with his life-giving teaching, he went even farther and declared that this manna is his own body and blood: "I am that living bread which has come down from heaven; if anyone eats this bread he shall live forever. Moreover, the bread which I will give is my own flesh; I give it for the life of the world" (6:51). When the listeners questioned what seemed to be an excessive statement, Jesus insisted, with even stronger language: "In truth, in very truth I tell you, unless you eat the flesh of the Son of Man and drink his blood you can have no life in you. Whoever eats my flesh and drinks my blood possesses eternal life, and I will raise him up on the last day" (6:53-54). It would be difficult to imagine a stronger or more explicit statement of the reality of the Eucharistic presence of Jesus for the nourishment of his followers.

What then is this new manna from heaven that Jesus provides for the journey through the wilderness? Is it his teaching, as indicated in verses 35-50, or is it his body and blood, as just stated? Actually, it is both, and to separate them or to set them against each other would be to distort this important message. To receive the Eucharistic body and blood of Jesus without truly accepting his teaching and living by it would be to misunderstand completely the meaning of that Eucharistic presence. For it is not a presence with magical power that will somehow save us in spite of ourselves.

In fact, Raymond Brown states that this may have been a problem already at the end of the first century and that John insisted on the importance of true, living faith to counter this magical tendency (*The Gospel According to John,* Vol. I, p. 290). Paul echoed the same concern when he warned the Corinthians that the Eucharist would be fruitful only for those who received it in the context of a life devoted to concern for others (1 Cor 11:17-34).

Thus it becomes clear that the manna which nourishes the Christian on the journey of faith and which enables hope to conquer cynicism and despair is the commitment to loving service. This is the heart of the teaching of Jesus and it is the deepest meaning of the Eucharistic manna. For the body and blood of the Lord in the Eucharist are a body broken for others and a blood poured out in sacrifice for others. To receive this sacrificial body and blood is to commit oneself unalterably to the loving service that they signify. Thus, a mysterious and wonderful bonding occurs between Jesus and the Christian, not just from receiving the Eucharist, but also from living the love and unselfishness of Jesus. "My flesh is real food; my blood is real drink. Whoever eats my flesh and drinks my blood dwells continually in me and I dwell in him" (6:55-56).

The journey through the wilderness is difficult because it means embracing the mystery of a life spent for others. But that also means becoming one with Jesus. This mystical union provides such a wealth of love and hope and joy that the journey is made on light feet and with shining eyes! "This is the bread which came down from heaven; and it is not like the bread which our fathers ate: they are dead, but whoever eats this bread shall live forever" (6:58). Paul also extols the experience of loving union with God that is the reward of those who wholeheartedly embrace the unselfish ideal of Jesus:

> For I am convinced that there is nothing in death or life, in the realm of spirits or superhuman powers, in the world as it is or the world as it shall be, in the forces of the universe, in heights or depths — nothing in all

creation that can separate us from the love of God in
Christ Jesus our Lord (Rom 8:38-39).

We have noted already that biblical revelation is received only
when we enter experientially into the saving events of the Bible.
The ultimate saving event is the passion, death and resurrection
of Jesus. To the extent that we are able to become participants in
that event through unselfish love and service, we also become one
with Jesus. The mystical union with the person of Jesus becomes
the ultimate and most perfect form of revelation, for Jesus is the
only truly adequate "word" of God. All other forms of revelation
are merely approximations and need to be constantly revised
and refined. Therefore, all biblical learning and conversion
point toward and are fully realized in personal communion
with Jesus.

ABBA, FATHER

It is easy to speak about being one with Jesus but this is such
a personal matter that it defies analysis or description. In this
case, as in every deeply personal experience, five minutes of the
experience is more revealing than five volumes of analysis. With
that warning in mind, it may nonetheless be helpful to point out
that being one with Jesus means to experience God as Jesus did,
namely, as loving Father. This happens, of course, in the human
nature which he shares with us and in which he speaks to us
about God. Some may be disturbed by this constant reference to
the relationship of Jesus to God as that of obedient Son to loving
Father because it seems to introduce the element of masculinity
into the basic model for the relationship of every Christian,
female or male, to God. This is undoubtedly due to the historical
fact that Jesus himself was a male. However, it is important to
note that the essential element in the relationship has nothing
to do with gender. It is the relationship between the one who
loves into being and freedom and the other who responds freely

and gratefully.

God is both masculine and feminine; response to God's love is both masculine and feminine. Neither is better or worse than the other. The limitations of human experience and language should not distract us from the real meaning of this relationship.

It is easy to say that we know God as Father and we say it constantly in our prayers but that is not the same as truly believing it. When we reflect on the fact that true awareness of God's parenting love would drive all fear out of our lives we realize also how lacking we still are in this trust. Saint Paul tells us that it is the work of the Holy Spirit to give us that deep experiential conviction of the Father's love: "To prove that you are sons [and daughters], God has sent into our hearts the Spirit of his Son, crying 'Abba! Father!'" (Gal 4:6).

> For all who are moved by the Spirit of God are sons [and daughters] of God. The Spirit you have received is not a spirit of slavery leading you back into a life of fear, but a Spirit that makes us sons [and daughters], enabling us to cry 'Abba! Father!' In that cry the Spirit of God joins with our spirit in testifying that we are God's children; and if children, then heirs (Rom 8:14-16).

The difficulty of believing that we are truly loved was brought home to me when I was on vacation once and my little nephew, Pat, asked me what I was doing when I read my breviary. I told him that l was thanking God for the sunshine and the rain and eagles and raccoons (knowing these were his favorite animals). Then I added, ". . . and for Pat." There was a long period of silence, and finally he said, "Pat who?" Saint Paul is saying that it is the task of the Spirit to convince us interiorly of our loveability, which is just another way of saying that God is good and truly cares for us.

This is what is really meant by the Good News, the gospel. One may memorize all the gospels, but if he does not feel loved he has not really heard the Good News! This good news is not just for a select few; it is for all without discrimination. Again

Saint Paul writes: "So he (Jesus) came and proclaimed the good news: peace to you who were far off, and peace to those who were near by; for through him we both alike have access to the Father in the one Spirit" (Eph 2:17-18). To have access to the Father is to discover the Father's goodness and love, a discovery that drives out fear, anxiety and insecurity. To know this love is to feel wanted, cherished, at home. "Thus you are no longer aliens in a foreign land, but fellow-citizens with God's people, members of God's household" (Eph 2:19).

A deeply experienced awareness of the Father's love not only provides freedom and confidence now; it also gives a profound sense of the promise that God has put in our future. The Spirit convinces us of God's present love and, at the same time, makes us aware of our pilgrim status by showing us that the full gift comes only at the end. Saint Paul sensed this perfectly:

> Up to the present, we know, the whole created universe groans in all its parts as if in the pangs of childbirth. Not only so, but even we, to whom the Spirit is given as first fruits of the harvest to come, are groaning inwardly while we wait for God to make us his sons [and daughters] and set our whole body free. For we have been saved, though only in hope (Rom 8:22-24).

Thus, the Spirit gives us a sense of confidence now but, at the same time, a deep feeling of homesickness as we yearn for what is still to be realized. It is in this context that we must understand Saint Paul's reference to the Spirit as "the pledge that we shall enter upon our heritage, when God has redeemed what is his own . . ." (Eph 1:14). The Spirit is the pledge or down-payment that guarantees the full gift in the Kingdom. Truly, then, the Spirit causes us to live in hope.

PRAYING IN THE SPIRIT

As we have noted before, the most perfect form of prayer is an expression of gratitude and praise for the goodness of God as experienced in his gracious deeds, in history and in our own lives. Since the Spirit is the one who convinces us, subtly but forcefully, of that goodness of the Father, to pray in the Spirit means to praise and thank God for the goodness we experience now but even more so for the goodness that is promised. Thus, the Spirit enables us to bless the future and thereby to turn its threat into promise. This creates in turn a spirit of joyful expectation that dispels the darkness of despair that can easily paralyze our creativity. The Spirit helps us to smile when others are gloomy and to expect the best when others prepare for the worst.

Anxiety about the future frequently drives people to some form of escape from a burden that seems too difficult to bear. In our day, this often takes the form of drug or alcohol abuse. Saint Paul wrote about this in the language of his own day:

> Do not give way to drunkenness and the dissipation that goes with it, but let the Holy Spirit fill you: speak to one another in psalms, hymns and songs; sing and make music in your hearts to the Lord; and in the name of our Lord Jesus Christ give thanks every day for everything to our God and Father (Eph 5:18-20).

This suggests that a large part of the solution to problems of escapism is to help its victims to discover the thrill of the Spirit who is able to convince them of the incredible reality of God's love. Mere condemnation and punishment may actually increase the need to escape. Those who can sing and make music in their hearts to the Lord have discovered how to be "high" in God's way — a way that leads to love, gentleness and peace.

The doorway to this spiritual enthusiasm is humble prayer. This may appear unpromising but we must keep in mind the words of Saint Paul in his letter to the Romans:

> . . . the Spirit comes to the aid of out weakness. We do not even know how we ought to pray, but through our inarticulate groans the Spirit himself is pleading for us,

> and God who searches our inmost being knows what
> the Spirit means, because he pleads for God's people in
> God's own way . . . (8:26-27).

Therefore, when we, like the Israelites, cry out from our own Egyptian bondage, we know that the Spirit, who is present throughout creation, cries out with us. Taken alone, our voice seems small and forlorn but when it is joined to the powerful voice of the Spirit it becomes a full-throated chorus that reaches to the throne of God.

Praying in the Spirit is, therefore, praying in hope. It is blessing the future so that the future may be exorcised of its demonic power to frighten and may instead be filled with promise — the promise that a good and merciful Creator has provided for us. This is, once again, the David-spirit of the Psalms. Our Saul-spirit would like us to be suspicious of the future and to dwell on its darkness so that we may join the unhappy but comfortable company of the purveyors of gloom and doom. But our David-spirit, supported by the all-powerful Spirit of God, can easily rout the negative forces if we will give it half a chance. Praying in the Spirit is, therefore, inseparable from living in hope.

7
Traveling Together

The journey of faith is a very personal adventure but it cannot be made alone. The reason for this is not difficult to discover. For this is no longer a journey through geographical territory such as the wilderness of Sinai. It is a spiritual journey of growth and conversion: it is leaving selfish behavior and moving toward unselfish love and service. It is also a journey through time, from a fairly normal egocentricity in childhood to a freely chosen and ever more generous concern for others in adulthood and then to a complete trust in the Lord in the uncertainties of old age. Since this journey is made or abandoned on the issue of selfishness, it must inevitably involve other people. The egocentric person remains alone, even though he may live in a crowded city; and the unselfish person lives with and is a gift to others, even though he lives in a remote hermit's cave. To make the biblical journey, then, is to walk with others, caring for them and being supported by them. This was the way that Jesus made the journey; there is no other way.

DIFFERENT MEMBERS, ONE BODY

The classic biblical text on the subject of Christian community is Saint Paul's first letter to the Corinthians, chapter twelve. There Paul compares community to the human body which, like community, has a variety of members with different abilities and functions yet manages to direct and organize these parts in a way that serves the purposes of the one body. Paul realizes, of course, that the members of a human body do not have free will; they may malfunction but they cannot disobey. Nonetheless, we sometimes speak of them as if they could obey or disobey. Thus, a lame person may say, "My leg just won't listen to me any more." Saint Paul attributes free will to bodily members also in order to make the comparison with community more realistic.

> A body is not one single organ, but many. Suppose the foot should say, 'Because I am not a hand, I do not belong to the body,' it does belong to the body none the less. Suppose the ear were to say, 'Because I am not an eye, I do not belong to the body,' it does still belong to the body. If the body were all eye, how could it hear? If the body were all ear, how could it smell? But, in fact, God appointed each limb and organ to its own place in the body, as he chose. If the whole were one single organ, there would not be a body at all; in fact, however, there are many different organs, but one body (1 Cor 12:14-20).

In a somewhat simplistic manner, Paul thus illustrates what is for him a primary principle, namely, that being different does not necessarily mean being inferior. In fact, as is quite evident in the case of the human body, variety represents wealth, not poverty. The body's abilities are greatly enhanced by various members, each with its own specialized function. Variety also increases beauty; a harmonious combination of colors is always more pleasing than one solid color. Why then should some members feel that they do not belong to the body? Why do they feel "left out?" Paul continues his analogy with those questions in mind.

> The eye cannot say to the hand, 'I do not need you'; nor the head to the feet, 'I do not need you.' Quite the contrary: those organs of the body which seem to be more frail than others are indispensable, and those parts of the body which we regard as less honorable are treated

> with special honor . . . But God has combined the various
> parts of the body, giving special honor to the humbler
> parts, so that there might be no sense of division in
> the body, but that all its organs might feel the same
> concern for one another. If one organ suffers, they all
> suffer together. If one flourishes, they all rejoice together
> (1 Cor 12:21-26).

If a particular member feels that it does not belong to the whole, it is simply because the other members have not shown their appreciation for it and for its contribution. It has been taken for granted and therefore ignored as if it had no needs of its own. This is clearly contrary to God's purpose for he intended that each member should receive the attention it needs from the other members. If that attention is lacking, there cannot fail to be division in the body. In this way, the body, and just as certainly the corresponding family or community, experiences true sickness. Neglected members begin to clamor for attention as their hurt becomes intolerable and those who have been neglectful resent these "demands" for attention because they interfere with their selfish and thoughtless habits. It is very easy to destroy the delicate balance of gift given and gift received. And when that balance is destroyed, it is very difficult to restore it. But when there is mutual respect and concern and thoughtfulness the resulting harmony is a joy on earth and praise in heaven!

It should be emphasized that most lack of harmony in community or family situations is probably caused by thoughtlessness rather than malice. When people are very busy or preoccupied they tend to ignore the small and seemingly useless gestures of gratitude or appreciation that are really very important. What is done wrongly is readily noted and criticized but what is done right is often left without any recognition. When I was rector of Saint Vincent Seminary I tried to make it a rule for myself that I would always compliment a student at least twice for every correction. I soon discovered that I found many reasons for complimenting students in situations where I would normally have ignored their achievements or taken them for granted. I tried to avoid also the "yes, but" practice of linking compliment with criticism and thereby negating it. I did not follow my rule in all cases, as former students will no doubt remember, but I remain convinced that it is a good rule and could make us all more conscious of the good in others and more effective in calling that good forth to the benefit of the entire community. This is such an important consideration because these words of appreciation are so easy to say and the resulting benefit is so great. The "hand" or the "foot" would be happy to do its work if the "eye" or the "head" would simply say, at regular intervals, how much they are needed and appreciated. They would thus be liberated to compliment and thank other members so that the whole body would be healthy and harmonious.

It does not require faith to recognize the value of gratitude and appreciation as a means for enabling people to do their best. Wise and shrewd employers have long since realized that such affirmation can dramatically increase productivity. There is certainly nothing wrong with helping people to be better at whatever they are doing. However, for the believer gratitude and appreciation are not limited to recognition of another's good work; it goes far beyond this and expresses joy and gratefulness for another person's very being and, at the center of that being, his or her mystery or uniqueness. God has given to every human being a special gift of personal mystery which is part of that person's inner freedom. This gift is far more valuable than anyone's ability to produce goods or services. It is called forth and enhanced by love. It needs to be reenforced by appreciation. It is a participation in the mystery of God and is almost certainly what is meant by the statement in the creation story that "God created man in his own image" (Gen 1:27).

This sense of one's personal mystery can be very weak in situations where love and appreciation are withheld. Such a person is deeply impoverished. He suffers from low self-esteem, is unsure of himself and cannot believe that he could be valued or cherished by others. He will therefore be experienced as a boring and uninteresting person who has lost his capacity to surprise others. This is a terrible waste for he really has a gift but it has remained undiscovered with the result that he is unhappy and the community to which he belongs is deprived of his unique contributions. Showing gratitude and appreciation is not therefore a matter of personal whim or convenience; it is a matter of life and death. If one rarely says Thanks or seldom remembers birthdays or anniversaries or never gives cut flowers, this cannot be dismissed lightly as forgetfulness or the sign of a busy person. This can be gravely sinful. It is also very foolish and shortsighted because it results in fewer gifts for everyone, including the neglectful person.

THE GIFTS OF THE SPIRIT

Perhaps the most notable feature of a human community is the extraordinary diversity of its members. Very few, if any, are good at everything; no one is really good for nothing. This fact can be seen as delightful or lamentable, depending on one's point of view. Some fear and resent what is different or unfamiliar; others find diversity challenging and interesting. There is no doubt that the Bible presents diversity of persons and gifts as a dominant characteristic of God's good and beneficent creation.

Saint Paul discusses this diversity and its benefits when he writes about the gifts of the Spirit. "There are varieties of gifts, but the same Spirit. There are varieties of service, but the same Lord. There are many forms of work, but all of them, in all men, are the work of the same God" (1 Cor 12:4-6). Paul sees the beautiful diversity among Christians, therefore, as an extension of the wonderful diversity among the Persons of the Trinity. The Spirit, in the passage cited, is the Holy Spirit, the Lord is Jesus, and God refers to the Father. In a certain very real sense, one can say that the untiring love of Father, Son and Spirit not only results in perfect unity as one God but also establishes more clearly their distinctiveness as Persons. Thus, for example, the Father's love for the Son enhances the uniqueness of the Son since the Father loves him precisely as Son; he loves his "difference," his distinctiveness. This makes it clear that diversity is not the real enemy of unity. The enemy of unity is hatred or simply lack of love. For love thrives on diversity and promotes it. The result is unity, not uniformity. Uniformity is a human creation; it is the "law and order" of Pharaoh's oppressive Egypt. A true Christian community will, therefore, be nervous about uniformity but it will celebrate and promote unity in diversity. In such a community, people will want each member to be truly unique. Fathers will not want their sons to be simple clones of themselves and teachers will delight in examination answers that show creativity and imagination and not just a memorized repetition from the text book.

Saint Paul goes on to provide a sampling of some of the important gifts in various members of the community.

> In each of us the Spirit is manifested in one particular way, for some useful purpose. One man, through the Spirit, has the gift of wise speech, while another, by the power of the same Spirit, can put the deepest knowledge into words. Another, by the same Spirit, is granted faith; another, by the one Spirit, gifts of healing, and another miraculous powers; another has the gift of prophecy, and another the ability to distinguish true spirits from false; yet another has the gift of ecstatic utterance of different kinds, and another the ability to interpret it. But all these gifts are the work of one and the same Spirit, distributing them separately to each individual at will (1 Cor 12:7-11).

There has been a great deal of discussion about the exact meaning of these gifts of the Spirit. It is my own conviction that they do not represent rare and extraordinary gifts of grace which we should welcome if they come our way but which we are not likely to experience. On the contrary, I would view them as natural talents, possessed in varying degrees by very ordinary people. They may remain undeveloped or they may blossom into truly extraordinary and beneficent gifts under certain favorable circumstances. This critically important environment that will cause these natural gifts to reach their full potential is a climate of loving affirmation. Within communities there is often a tendency toward destructive competition. In such a competitive atmosphere, one member will see another's gift as a threat to his own self-confidence and will tend to minimize or ridicule its importance. In this way, he can stunt the development of that gift with a consequent impoverishment of its bearer as well as of the community for which the gift is intended. This attitude can become typical of a community and then it becomes almost impossible for individual gifts to flourish as hypercriticism replaces loving affirmation and the community engages in a kind of spiritual suicide.

On the other hand, where loving affirmation is the dominant and typical attitude of a community, new gifts will be constantly discovered and fostered, self-doubt and fear of testing one's gifts will be dispelled, seemingly unpromising members will surprise everyone with their contributions and all will be constantly enriched. When this happens, the Spirit is active in each individual for the benefit of all: "in each of us the Spirit is manifested in one particular way, for some useful purpose" (1 Cor 12:7). The gifts that Saint Paul mentions are examples of these individual gifts — the insight of wisdom, a special facility for expression, a unique clarity of faith, the healing touch. The "miraculous powers" would seem to be an obvious exception. However, a literal translation reads, "workings of powers" which does not necessarily imply anything miraculous. What this means is somewhat obscure but I would take it to refer to a unique talent for inspiring others to cooperate in community projects or something of that nature. Other examples are the gift of prophetic sensitivity for divine mystery, the discernment of a wise counsellor, the joyful exclamations called "speaking in tongues" and the "translation" of these joyful sounds into praise of God. This is only a sampling of the wonderful wealth and diversity of human gifts which can wonderfully enrich a community when called forth by love and appreciation.

LOVE, THE PERFECT GIFT

After speaking of the gifts of the Spirit and noting that they cannot be recognized or developed without a favorable environment, Saint Paul turns to a description of a superior or master gift: "And now I will show you the best way of all" (1 Cor 12:31). This "best way" refers to the special gift of love: "I may speak in tongues of men or of angels, but if I am without love, I am a sounding gong or a clanging cymbal" (1 Cor 13:1). All one's efforts amount to superficial sham and pretense if they are not expressions of love. This is very similar to what Paul means when he says that good works have no value without faith (Rom 3:28). Faith discovers the goodness and love of God and thus makes it possible to be truly good oneself and to love unselfishly. In this way, good works are a product and sign of faith and love, but it is the faith and love that make one a child of God and heir of the Kingdom. In fact, good works without faith and love can be a source of pride and lead to sin. No wonder then that Saint Paul calls it "the best way of all" (1 Cor 12:31).

What Paul means by love in this context is far removed from what is often suggested by that word in our own popular culture. For Paul, love is essentially unselfish. It is not a yearning to possess another person nor is it based on another's attractiveness. It is an expression of goodness and seeks only the benefit of the other person even if this means "losing" that person. False love wants the other to be dependent; true love seeks the other's freedom — even the freedom to fly away! What makes true love possible is not the attractiveness of the other but the goodness in oneself, a goodness discovered because one has been loved — loved by others and ultimately by God. One becomes a truly loving person by opening oneself to love and goodness, and then freely choosing to pass that love on to others. One must be a loved person before one can be a loving one.

Thus, the ability to love truly is the most important gift of all. When it is present, the gifts of others are seen with a clear eye and called forth in a proper and effective way. When it is absent, the gifts of others will be viewed selfishly and will either be denied and rejected or be called forth in a self-interested way. Saint Paul sees true love, then, as that special environment in which personal gifts can be discovered and can blossom and flourish to full potential. It is the heart and soul of a truly Christian community. In fact, it is the presence of the Spirit in that community. For the Spirit is the Spirit of love who enables people to become like Christ, that is, truly unselfish and loving persons.

Saint Paul goes on then to list the characteristics of this special gift of love. One should note two things in particular about these qualities of true love: first, they are not at all romantic or centered in emotion and, second, they all presuppose some freedom and confidence in the one who loves, which means that he has himself been loved. All of the passages that follow are from chapter thirteen of Paul's first letter to the Corinthians.

"Love is patient" (v 4). Literally, love is "large-souled"; it makes room for others and welcomes their differences; it is hospitable and ecumenical; it does not feel threatened or diminished by new or unfamiliar gifts. "Love is kind" (v 4). Literally, it is "useful," that is, it is helpful and constructive; it views life positively and expects to find goodness; it is not parasitical or draining; it nourishes others and makes them stronger. "[Love] envies no one" (v 4). True love does not blight or spoil the gifts of others by wishing they did not have them or by making them feel guilty about their good fortune. Rather, it genuinely rejoices in their gifts. This is possible because the one who loves knows that he too has gifts and is therefore free to rejoice in the blessings of others. Moreover, it knows instinctively that all benefit from gifts appreciated and that all suffer from gifts denied.

"Love is never boastful" (v 4). The Greek original suggests an attempt to draw attention to oneself by various kinds of self-promotion. This comes from insecurity or lack of confidence. Such a person feels the need to call attention to himself lest he be totally ignored and become in a sense non-existent. True love is calm, confident and self-possessed; it presupposes the liberating experience of having been loved.

"Nor (is love) conceited" (v 4). Literally, love is not "puffed up" or arrogant. This is another way of dealing with insecurity. Instead of noisy self-promotion, one resorts to a feigned and haughty independence. It is a desperate stratagem for it tries to ignore what it needs most of all. Once again, true love presupposes a sense of confidence, an inner freedom.

"Nor (is love) rude" (v 4). True love is very sensitive about those formalities that make people feel comfortable and secure. It avoids unseemly or improper behavior, not because it wants to be formal or stilted, but because such behavior makes people nervous and robs them of the peace that they deserve. Thus, love will respect proper etiquette simply because it is a way of showing one's respect and regard for others. More formal dress and polite behavior are important ways of telling another that he or she is valued and respected. "(Love is) never selfish" (v 5). The original text reads: "Love does not seek what is its own." True love is not preoccupied with self or with its own interests. It is not self-conscious and defensive. It feels secure at home and so is able to reach out to others. It is not overly concerned about making mistakes or being misunderstood or appearing awkward. Rather, it acts spontaneously, like David dancing before the ark; it is generous and free and natural.

"(Love is) not quick to take offense" (v 5). This may be the most revealing of all the characteristics of true love. It is not hypersensitive and does not offend others by making them feel guilty for supposed injuries. There is always a great temptation, especially if one lives with reasonably sensitive people, to "punish" them by feigning injury, even when it is clear that injury was not intended. Such people walk around wearing "signs" that read "Fragile," "Handle With Care," "Artist in Residence"! This is an unloving thing to do because it causes everyone to be cautious and guarded; it destroys spontaneity and peace. It is also dangerous because it is the beginning of that destructive refuge of self-pity. When a person begins to blame others and to indulge in self-pity he is turning away from growth and conversion; he is rejecting God's call to journey.

"Love keeps no score of wrongs" (v 5). Closely allied to self-pity is the tendency to nurse old injuries, real or imagined. True love realizes that no one can go through life without being hurt or offended occasionally. But it does not magnify and cling to these experiences and use them as excuses for avoiding hard decisions or hard work. In other words, it does not produce a Saul-figure, who expects evil and makes the most of it. Rather, like David, it lets evil go and clings to the good in life; it avoids excuses and accepts responsibility; it counts its blessings and tries to forgive and forget the hurts in life. Once again, true love presupposes being loved and freed; it uses that freedom to choose properly.

"(Love) does not gloat over other men's sins, but delights in the truth" (v 6). Love does not draw comfort from the misfortunes of others because it does not view others as rivals or competitors. The one who truly loves is sufficiently secure so that the success or good fortune of others is not seen as a threat. Rather, it is a cause for joy and celebration. True love is optimistic about life with its ups and downs. It is not paranoid; it does not see conspiracies everywhere. It is Davidic in its trust of God's world and God's people.

"There is nothing love cannot face; there is no limit to its faith, its hope, and its endurance" (v 7). This is a rather free translation of a difficult Greek text. One may argue about the details but the general meaning is clear enough: True love is victorious over all the negative and destructive forces in human life. It is endlessly optimistic because it is in touch with the all-powerful love of God. It is a hidden and surprising strength that seems to thrive on adversity and is strongest when there seems to be no longer any place for faith and hope and perseverance. This kind of love is far removed from that romantic attachment that is destroyed by the slightest imperfection. This kind of love conquers all because it is giving, not receiving, and because it is part of the infinite giving of God.

This wonderful and irresistible power of love is the ultimate treasure in human life. Those who possess it are very rich; those who lack it are desperately poor. It cannot be bought or taken; it is a pure gift. But it is a gift that is offered to all. In order to receive it, one must be open to the gift that is in life; one must look for flowers and drink in all their beauty; one must count blessings and dismiss woes. This readiness for the gift in life will give strength and freedom to choose to be gift to others. The one gifted thus chooses to become gift. To be a gift is far from easy; indeed, it can be very painful but it is the only valid purpose of human existence and leads ultimately to happy community and profound peace.

THE LORD'S PRAYER

The power of love comes from the fact that it is a participation in the ultimate power of God. In order to tap this infinite reservoir of divine power, human creatures must maintain vital contact with God. This contact is established by faith and sustained by prayer. The disciples noticed that Jesus derived significant strength and peace from his moments of quiet prayer and they wished to discover the secret of this spiritual refreshment. "Once, in a certain place, Jesus was at prayer. When he ceased, one of his disciples said, 'Lord, teach us to pray . . . ' " (Luke 11:1). The response of Jesus to this request is the Lord's prayer. It is the only prayer explicitly recommended by Jesus himself and occupies therefore a unique and unparalleled place of importance among the myriad forms of prayer. It should be the object of constant study and reflection. Every nuance of this prayer of prayers should be carefully noted and cherished. Saint Teresa of Avila understood this perfectly when, in response to a request for instruction in the art of contemplative prayer, she is said to have replied simply: "Recite the Our Father . . . but do so very slowly."

One of the best studies of the Lord's prayer is an article by Raymond Brown in *Theological Studies* (22, 175-208) entitled: "The Pater Noster as an Eschatological Prayer." In this article, Brown highlights the frequently overlooked eschatological orientation of this prayer. By this he means that the prayer is concerned primarily with the end of time, understood in the biblical sense as a powerful magnetism that draws all things toward the future and reveals the meaning of history only at its end. In this sense, it is a prayer for travellers. Moreover, since it is addressed to "our" Father, it is a prayer for those who travel together; it is a community prayer. In the gospels, only Jesus speaks of "my" Father; when his disciples address the Father, it must always be in the plural. This practice emphasizes the uniqueness of Jesus' relationship to the Father but it also suggests strongly the impossibility of a purely private kind of religion; we are in this together and we, to a large extent, are saved or lost together!

Luke's version of the Lord's prayer (11:2-4) is somewhat shorter than Matthew's (6:9-13). Following the principle that the shorter of two versions is the more ancient (since one would be inclined to add to, rather than to subtract from, the original), it is assumed that Matthew expanded Luke's version. Since Matthew's version is the one that is found in the liturgy and piety of Christian churches, it will be used in the explanation that follows. Significant differences from Luke's version will be noted at the appropriate places.

The most important word in the Lord's prayer is the word "Father" (6:9). This is so true that the prayer can be either a meaningless recitation or a rich and deeply personal experience depending on how one understands the Fatherhood of God. There is no doubt that this word, "Father," is in some ways imperfect and inadequate. It is after all a human word and must therefore be "purified" of some of its merely human connotations, such as masculinity, when it is applied to God. The two characteristics of fatherhood that make it appropriate for expressing the human experience of God are the qualities of strength and goodness. Human fathers are generally stronger than their children just as God is obviously much stronger than all his creatures. Ideally, human fathers are also good, kind, generous and protective. They love their children and help them to find identity and grow toward responsible freedom. God is supremely good and loving. When he is addressed as "Father," it is primarily his liberating love and goodness that are affirmed. It is relatively easy to declare

God's strength; it is far more difficult to affirm his goodness when we mean by that not just a theoretical fact but a personally experienced reality.

This becomes especially difficult when one's experience of human fatherhood has been negative or when one has never known a human father. In such cases, one should understand "father" as the person who has been the primary source of liberating love in one's life. This may well be one's mother, or grandparent or even a dear friend; or it may be a combination of persons. Thus, from the springboard of a human experience of love joined to strength, we are asked to leap toward the infinite strength and most tender and liberating love of God, our good Father. Though our experience of God may not yet match all the implications of Father, we are asked to refer to God constantly as Father in the hope that we will gradually find our experience catching up to our words. That is why the traditional Latin introduction to the Lord's prayer in the Eucharist reads " . . . We dare to say: Our Father . . ." It is as if the discovery of God as loving Father is too good to be true and can be affirmed only with the help of the Church's insistent urging.

Thus, there is a special victory of faith over appearances in our discovery of the wonderfully comforting fatherhood of God. For God is the ultimate mystery and accordingly is, at least potentially, the source of much dread and anxiety for his struggling human creatures. But faith enables us to find the goodness hidden in mystery, and nowhere more than in the supreme mystery that is God. As faith illuminates the mystery in our lives, we become "friends of mystery," ready for happy surprise, finding meaning in what we do not understand far more than in what we can "control" with our knowledge. Accordingly, when we declare in faith that the impenetrable mystery of God is really our loving Father, we are also greeting every stranger as friend, and blessing all the hidden power of the universe, and declaring good and promising the darkness of the future where the Father awaits us in our true homeland. Our natural fear and uncertainty about the future is thus replaced with joyful expectation of rich inheritance.

Having made (and hopefully having believed) the daring assertion of God's loving fatherhood, we go on (in Matthew's version) to say that he is "our" Father (6:9). The clear implication is that it is impossible to declare the fatherly goodness of the divine mystery and otherness without also asserting the brotherly and sisterly goodness of the mystery and otherness of our fellow human beings. Thus, there is a strict parallelism between one's attitude toward God and toward other persons, so that calling God Father implies calling other persons brothers and sisters. This accounts for a happy reciprocation by which one discovers the goodness of God through the loving witness of a brother or sister and then, strengthened by that discovery, is able to return that love to more and more fellow human beings. For, as we are ever more enriched by our experience of God's goodness, we can put away that destructive competition which is the source of so much human dissension. We become so rich in the Father's goodness that we can afford to be generous, tolerant, patient and forgiving toward all.

This God who is loving Father is said to be "in heaven" (6:9). In the popular imagination, heaven is generally pictured as a place of bliss, high above the earth and far removed from earthly miseries. Though the Bible does occasionally represent heaven in this way, it is far more common to see it pictured in the temporal mode as a time of peace and happiness at the end of history. It is reserved for those who have made the journey through history in a manner that is faithful to the revelations of the Creator who set history on its course. From this perspective, heaven is not so much high above the earth as it is in the radical future, in the *eschaton*. When we address God therefore as our Father "in heaven," we should not picture him as one enthroned in some high place but as one who is at the end of the journey welcoming with open arms his children as they enter into their true homeland. The goodness of the Father is experienced, then, not only as loving care in the present, but perhaps even more as bright promise for the future. As we grow older, this prayer should direct our attention more and more toward the gracious welcome that awaits us just beyond the momentary darkness of death. By adding "our" and "in heaven" to "Father,"

Matthew thus simply draws out two important implications of God's fatherhood.

The remainder of the Lord's prayer is very carefully and neatly arranged in two groups of three petitions. All six petitions are addressed to God, our Father, but the first three concern God and the latter three concern us and our needs. The petitions about God are really three ways of asking for one thing, namely, the full revelation of God's goodness at the end of time. They are expressed in Semitic terminology which needs translation: "thy name be hallowed" (Matt 6:9) requests that God's name or reputation be fully vindicated. The verb is in the Greek aorist tense which conveys a definitive nuance that cannot be easily captured in English. This final and definitive vindication of God's holiness occurs only at the end of the world when all secrets will be revealed. In effect, therefore, this is an earnest plea for that final accounting when it will be clear that God, who has been blamed for so much in the course of history, will be clearly seen as consistently good, gracious and loving. To pray for the end of the world because that is the time of God's triumph is an act of profound trust for a human being who instinctively fears the end of time.

The second petition, "thy kingdom come" (6:10), has essentially the same meaning. In the biblical context, the word "kingdom" does not carry the overtones of human kingship where power and domination are often the prevalent features, especially in the light of so many autocratic or tyrannical human kings. Biblical kingship ideally represented power only for salvation and protection. God's kingdom then is his plan for the salvation, liberation and protection of all those who have put their trust in him. When Jesus announced the coming of God's kingdom he was saying that God would henceforth be present in a special new way to provide for his children. In a very real sense, one could say that God's kingdom is, quite simply, God's dream for us all, much as any good father cherishes dreams for his children. In this petition, then, we declare our trust in God's goodness as we ask that his dreams for us be realized, definitively, at the end of time. Thus, in faith we affirm our conviction that God controls the end of our lives and of history and that can only be a happy prospect.

The third petition is found in Matthew's version alone: "thy will be done, on earth as in heaven" (6:10). The meaning, once again, is essentially the same as in the previous petitions. The verb is again in the definitive aorist tense and so the accomplishment of God's will is seen, not as obedience here and now, but as an event of the last days when God's will, that is, his gracious plan and design, will be finally and perfectly brought to fruition. This divine design embraces all of reality, whether in heaven or on earth. Thus, in these petitions, God's name and kingdom and will are virtually synonymous. Though we desire, in our human wisdom, to extend our lives and push back the end of time as long as possible, we declare in our wisdom of faith that we trust this good Father so much that the fulfillment of his gracious plan becomes more important than the extension of an uncertain human existence. Once again, we are asked to say more than we may at any given moment be able to accept in the hope that our experience will gradually catch up to our faith-inspired vision.

The second half of the Lord's prayer is also made up of three petitions addressed to the Father. However, they are concerned with the needs of Christians. The first of this latter group of petitions expresses the need for nourishment on the journey toward that heavenly homeland where the Father awaits his children. "Give us today our daily bread" (6:11). This is not the bread needed for bodily food. It is the daily "manna" of hope and courage that make it possible to survive and to move ahead in the wilderness. The hardships of the journey are tolerable only as long as the yearning for the goal is strong. When the goal no longer seems worthwhile the traveller is ready to turn back to a more comfortable and comprehensible way of life. Thus, the first and indispensable nourishment for the journey is the motivation and encouragement provided by a deep sense of hope. The Christian who yearns for the homecoming and for rest with the Father must be concerned about perseverance on the journey and so he earnestly begs for this primary nourishment.

This meaning of the "daily bread" becomes even more explicit if we are aware of an alternate and more probable translation of the Greek original for "daily." The Greek verbal adjective involved is in fact ambiguous. It can be derived from either a verb meaning "to be present" or from another verb meaning "to come to be." In the former case, "daily" is a good translation; in the second instance, the proper rendering in English would be "future." The petition then would read: "Give us today our future bread" or "our bread for tomorrow," which is, of course, our bread of hope. This latter translation, though unfamiliar, is probably accurate. In effect, therefore, the Christian recognizes the aching void of his unfulfillment and senses that the Father's loving call from the future is a summons to rest at home. But the journey of unselfish service is difficult and often seems unproductive. Hence, the need to pray constantly, as Jesus urges, for the daily manna of courage and hope and perseverance.

The second petition that expresses the need of the Christian traveler is concerned with forgiveness: "Forgive us the wrong we have done, as we have forgiven those who have wronged us" (6:12). Anyone who has traveled extensively will recognize the importance of limiting one's baggage. The wise traveler always travels lightly. This is true also of the spiritual journey of faith where the baggage is the awful burden of guilt and remorse. We may have been able to suppress much of this sense of guilt but it continues to weigh us down in our subconscious where it is insidiously damaging to the joy and spontaneity needed for a successful journey. This sense of guilt can erode our morale to the point where we are virtually paralyzed and immobilized. Small wonder then that this concern for freedom from guilt ranks second only to the paramount concern for nourishment.

The verb "forgive" is once again in the definitive aorist tense. It refers therefore to more than the simple act of forgiving occasional, obvious sins; it suggests a deep permanent sense of being forgiven, of being liberated, of "feeling" forgiven. And this experience of forgiveness extends beyond the realm of personal sins to include our shortcomings and weaknesses, which can also discourage us on our journey. Thus, we ask the Father to make us know that it is all right to be short or tall, fat or thin, bald or curly-haired! It is a plea for liberation on every level so that we may run the path of loving service unencumbered, with wings on our feet and a song in our hearts. In return for this extraordinary favor, we solemnly promise to forgive others — for their sins, for their short-comings and failings, for their tendency to annoy and frustrate us. We promise to use our precious freedom to be generous, compassionate and understanding toward our fellow-travelers.

It is almost impossible to exaggerate the importance of this matter of mutual forgiveness. A hypercritical and judgmental person may be able to put on the appearance of a faithful Christian but he is infected with the near fatal malady of the Pharisees who are best known as those who wasted the greatest opportunity ever offered to man. No one appeared more ready for the Messiah than they were; no one was as blind as they were when the Messiah came! On this point Jesus was absolutely clear and unyielding. Only those who are ready to forgive others from their hearts will be admitted to the Kingdom. Those who nurse grudges or refuse to speak to others or make no effort to reconcile differences will find all their virtue wasted. For, while they withhold forgiveness from others, they are determining how God will act toward them on the day of judgment. It is hardly an accident that we read the following warning immediately after the Lord's prayer in Matthew's gospel: "For if you forgive others the wrongs they have done, your heavenly Father will also forgive you; but if you do not forgive others, then the wrongs you have done will not be forgiven by your Father" (6:14-15). The matter could not have been put more starkly and challengingly!

The final petition of the Lord's prayer is hardly more than a postscript and, in fact, its second half is missing from Luke's version. It is concerned with that dark, turbulent moment that comes near the end of the journey and which can cast a shadow of fear and anxiety back over one's life of faith. "And do not bring us to the test, but save us from the evil one" (6:13). In the original Greek, it is clear that the "temptation" of the first part of this petition is not what we usually mean by temptation, that is, an enticement to sin. Rather, it is the moment of testing, of sifting and screening and evaluating that comes at the end of life. This petition does not really ask to be spared this test; that is impossible. Thus, on the one hand, we declare our awareness and acceptance of the fact of the final struggle. On the other hand, we want to make it clear that we can deal honestly with the final struggle only because we count on the Lord's presence and help. Thus, it becomes a reminder of the living presence of God at that final and decisive moment of our lives.

The second half of the petition is also concerned with that final moment of darkness. Although the Greek is ambiguous and allows the possibility of both "evil" and "evil one," the latter translation is generally favored. For the one who is seen behind all tests of faith is Satan or the evil one. The Christian asks that the Lord may be present in the darkness to safeguard his faith and strengthen his resolve so that the devil's suggestions of despair may be resisted and rejected. Thus, this final petition situates the believer in a happy middle position between a morbid preoccupation with death which prevents attention to present living and a denial of the fact of death that can lead to cruel surprise.

All of the petitions of the Lord's prayer are made in the light of the Father's tender love. As we repeat these petitions, reverently and thoughtfully, we are reminded of that love and are thus gradually liberated from the fear and discouragement and guilt that can make our journey so difficult. This is then the perfect prayer; it is a traveler's song — a song sung at times through tears, but joyful and buoyant nonetheless.

LESSONS FROM THE COMMUNITY OF JOHN

Saint Paul makes it clear that there can be no real Christian community without the loving affirmation of individual gifts. The Lord's prayer of Matthew and Luke emphasizes the importance of the Father's love for sustenance on the journey of faith. The gospel and letters of John give us much food for thought on the delicate issue of the proper place of authority and structure in a community shaped and animated by the Holy Spirit. Raymond Brown has presented an insightful and persuasive account of the development and fortunes of the community behind the gospel of John in his book, *The Community of the Beloved Disciple*. This community appears to have been originally very much like the other early Christian communities, namely, a congregation made up primarily of converts from Judaism who saw their new faith as a fulfillment of their Jewish beliefs (and hence would never have considered themselves "converts") and who saw in Jesus the promised Messiah. They would have believed firmly in the divinity of Jesus but would have expressed that faith in terms that were traditional and sufficiently ambiguous that they did not offend their Jewish compatriots. This so-called "low Christology" is typical of much of the language of the Synoptic gospels. For reasons that are not altogether clear, this community moved beyond this rather conservative and traditional position and began to speak so clearly about the divinity of Jesus that their Jewish neighbors, grounded in rigid monotheism, found their beliefs scandalous and offensive. This so-called "high Christology" is typical of the gospel of John where Jesus appears to be virtually omniscient and where he is heard to say such things as " . . . before Abraham was born, I am" (John 8:58). Although it is impossible to identify all the elements that influenced this development, one major and decisive factor was the mystical tendencies of the leader of this community whom the fourth gospel calls the Beloved Disciple. His intuitive grasp of the meaning of Jesus enabled him to see all reality in a profoundly symbolic way. Thus, the gospel of John is intended to reveal the true meaning behind the facade of worldly events as Jesus first presents miracles or "signs" and then becomes himself the ultimate sign, lifted high on the cross, to show that human life is for love and sacrifice and that these alone lead to glory.

Apparently, this mystical and rather radical development caused this community to be isolated from the more conservative communities and to be rejected outright by Judaism. This would account for the strong anti-Jewish tone of the fourth Gospel, where opposition to Jesus is attributed, not to the scribes and Pharisees as in the Synoptics, but simply to the Jews. It seems evident that the author of the gospel is collapsing the time gap between Jesus and the later community so that the community's experience becomes the experience of Jesus. This kind of identification would have been especially easy for a mystically oriented group. In any case, this community emerges as a group that is characterized by great warmth and intimacy within and by a certain fear and suspicion toward outsiders who at best misunderstand and at worst oppose it.

One must admire and may even envy the emphasis on love and intimacy that is so evident in the gospel of John. There are no references to structure, no mention of the power of the keys (as in Matthew 16:19) and it seems that the guidance of the community left by Jesus is entrusted entirely to the Paraclete, the Holy Spirit (John 14:16; 16:13-14). The preferred image of the church is not that of a structured building established on a rock but the more amorphous concept of branches drawing life from a vine. In fact, Raymond Brown concludes: "The Fourth Gospel is best interpreted as voicing a warning against the dangers inherent in such institutional developments by stressing what for the author is truly essential, namely, the living presence of Jesus in the Christian through the Paraclete" (*The Community of the Beloved Disciple*, p.88). This ideal of a community that downplays visible structure of authority and relies almost entirely on the Spirit is most attractive. However, as the letters of John reveal, it may also be impractical, utopian and at times disastrous.

In the letters of John we witness a community that is torn by dissension and conflict. It is not easy to sort out all the issues since we hear from only the side represented by the anonymous author. It is clear, however, that both sides claimed the Spirit and that there was no effective process available for adjudicating the dispute and reconciling the parties. The very fact that these letters were accepted as inspired Scripture indicates that the opposition of their author was accepted as the authentic interpretation of the fourth gospel by the Church. Raymond Brown, commenting on these letters of John, points out the important implications:

> The very fact that a Paraclete-centered ecclesiology had offered no real protection against schismatics ultimately caused his (the author's) followers to accept the authoritative presbyter-bishop teaching structure which in the second century became dominant in the Great Church but which was quite foreign to Johannine tradition (*The Community of the Beloved Disciple*, p. 146).

However, the sadder but wiser remnant of that community did not come to the more conservative and structured church empty-handed. They brought the riches of a high Christology which is still the typical Christology of that church. (See Brown: *The Community of the Beloved Disciple*, p.90.) They also brought a mystical perspective which is needed to correct and balance the very real danger of authoritarian and legalistic tendencies in the Christian church.

It is precisely this balance of the structural and the charismatic elements in the church that is essential if that church is to be truly a community that nourishes faith and represents love. This is true, not only of the church as a whole, but perhaps even more importantly of the myriad communities, from parish councils to great religious Orders, that make up the church. We have all heard about, or even felt, the suffering caused by a rigid and insensitive system of authority that seems to victimize even those leaders who want to be more humane. This suffering is very real and the danger of this excess is very great. At the same time, however, we should be aware of the danger of an amorphous kind of community that is unable to deal with problems and resolve conflicts. Rule by consensus sounds wonderful in theory but too often it means simply rule by the dominant personality in the group, which rule more often than not will result in something other than the common good. The ideal is a blend of essential structure and order with genuine humility and sensitivity to the Spirit who promotes

God's order — an order that finds room for everyone. This balance is never easy to achieve but its blessings are so obvious that we should never cease striving for it.

Part Three:

The Homecoming

INTRODUCTION

Jesus began his public ministry in a way that warmed the hearts of his followers. He spoke and acted like a true Messiah. Miracles flowed from his fingertips; he preached confidently and eloquently; he made the Old Testament prophets look good. But then he seemed to throw away all that power and promise of victory. His words became more and more obscure and his miracles were fewer and then ceased altogether. He went up to Judea and entered a cloud of mystery. He let go of everything that had seemed so promising; he became incredibly vulnerable; only his loving was the same or even greater. We who know the outcome cannot possibly imagine how disconcerting and tragic this all was to his disciples. We can begin to understand it only when our own lives suddenly make little sense as we face an unexpected and tragic event . . . and ultimately when we begin to die. Then we will know that Jesus was making room for God and for God's mysterious and wonderful plan. Then we will know in faith that we are letting go of our own plans and hopes to allow God to bring us to our true homeland in his gracious way and at his chosen moment. This homecoming, then, is made up of two acts: the first is a letting go which is the hardest and demands the most of us; the second is the arrival at home which is God's work and God's special gift. This letting go and arriving at home is the subject of that climax of all the gospels: the Passion, Death and Resurrection of Jesus. It is the final victory of love.

8
Letting Go

GETHSEMANE

The Passion Narrative is the climax and the most important part of all the gospels because it shows Jesus putting into practice what he had been preaching. It is true, of course, that he had exemplified the meaning of loving service in his public ministry but the deepest and fullest meaning of such loving service was revealed only in the last days of his human life. Though the four gospels differ considerably in their accounts of the public ministry, they are surprisingly similar in the Passion Narrative. We will draw our references from the gospel of Mark, the oldest of all the gospel stories.

One senses that things were now coming to a head: the chief priests and scribes had already decided that Jesus must be eliminated (14:1) and Jesus certainly knew that obedience to his mission was taking him into the jaws of death. In the intimacy of the final Passover meal with his disciples, he tried to prepare them for this by identifying himself with that sacrifice under the signs of bread-broken and wine-poured-out. Then he led them out to the garden of Gethsemane where he would confront and struggle with this terrible awareness of the imminence of death.

"When they reached a place called Gethsemane, he said to his disciples, 'Sit here while I pray' " (14:32). This was certainly not the first time that Jesus had withdrawn from the disciples to enter into communion with his Father. "And he took Peter and James and John with him" (14:33). Jesus had a closer relationship with these three disciples; they seemed to be kindred spirits who would understand his more personal experiences, such as the transfiguration (9:2). In this carefully crafted account, we are supposed to notice that Jesus was moving into an ever more private and personal world.

"Horror and dismay came over him, and he said to them, 'My heart is ready to break with grief; stop here and stay awake'" (14:34). The language here is very strong. It is as if Jesus had been able to ward off this moment with small distractions but then the dam broke and the awareness of imminent suffering, darkness and death rushed over him like a flood. Even the kindred spirits could not share this, and so he moved away from them to be alone in the struggle with his fate.

> Then he went forward a little, threw himself on the ground, and prayed that, if it were possible, this hour might pass him by. 'Abba, Father,' he said, 'all things are possible to thee; take this cup away from me. Yet not what I will, but what thou wilt.' (14:35-36).

Jesus moved away from the disciples as he entered the private sanctuary of his inner truth where there could be no play-acting but only reality. There, he was at first overwhelmed by the prospect of imminent and unavoidable death. Responding to the deep human instinct for survival, he begged his heavenly Father to postpone this terrible day. The "cup" symbolized his destiny and he asked that it be modified to give him more time. But then his faith took over and he said, in effect, "Father, I know that you love me and can will only what is good for me. I accept your will. It is perfectly all right if you want me to die tomorrow!" In a very real sense, this was the most crucial moment in the whole life of Jesus, for it was at this moment that he died on the all-important psychological and spiritual planes. Here he finally and totally rejected illusion or evasion and embraced the reality and truth of human life. He did so purely and simply because he had come to know and trust God as his loving Father, in spite of all appearances.

In contemplating the profound implications of Jesus' Gethsemane experience, we must not make the mistake of assuming that, because he was divine, he was only pretending to be filled with dismay. The fine Dominican scholar, Pierre Benoit, addresses this point:

> In his human nature, Jesus can and does ask God to spare him this suffering . . . We must not make him a 'pretender,' someone who in everything, from his birth to his death, merely pretends to escape, pretends to question, and so on. (*The Passion and Resurrection of Jesus Christ*, pp. 10-11).

In John's gospel, with its emphasis on the divinity of Jesus, there is no Gethsemane scene, but we must certainly prefer the earlier and historically more reliable accounts found in the Synoptic gospels where the humanity of Jesus is clearly and forcefully portrayed.

"He came back and found them asleep; and he said to Peter, 'Asleep, Simon? Were you not able to stay awake for one hour?' " (14:37). The drowsiness of the disciples was meant to illustrate how far removed they were from the experience of Jesus: they could not keep their eyes open while he was never more wide awake in his whole life! Their eyes were closed but his eyes were like saucers as he stared at the ultimate realities. There is a profound symbolism here. When a human being enters into the experience of dying he cannot take his friends with him; it is a profoundly personal and private experience. Yet he cannot really cope with it alone and so needs to turn, as Jesus did, to the One who alone can be present at such a time. It is at this moment, when we begin to die, that we will discover the true quality of our relationship to God.

" 'Stay awake, all of you; and pray that you may be spared the test. The spirit is willing but the flesh is weak' "(14:38). These words of Jesus were meant to be heard by all his followers. They remind us that the time we have prior to death must not be devoted so exclusively to the concerns of this world that we do not have time to discover the Father and to become true friends with him. When Jesus said that we must "stay awake" or "watch" and "pray," he was warning us of the danger of pushing God to the fringes of our lives with the result that, when we need him most, he will still be largely a stranger to us. Our present life is, therefore, more than anything else, a time for getting to know and to love and to be at home with God. We do this mostly by taking time to be with the Lord in prayer. Those who have in this way become friends of God and of his mystery will be able to face the "test," the ordeal of dying. They will not be betrayed by their human weakness but will grow strong in the courage of faith. Christian watchfulness is, therefore, a constant moving away from illusory appearances which suggest that life is for acquiring power and dominating others; it is moving toward the reality of a life devoted to love, responsibility and service in preparation for the coming of the Lord.

In his Gethsemane experience, Jesus "let go" of his sleeping disciples who could not follow him into his final agony. He turned instead to God as Abba, loving Father, and moved resolutely into the dark mystery of his final sacrifice. But there was a fire in those thick clouds — the fire and warmth of the Father's unfailing love for him. In that love, he would find his beloved disciples once again. But for the moment he must leave them or risk losing them forever. Everything and everyone, except God, must be released, when the time comes, so that in God they may be found again.

APOCALYPTIC CONSCIOUSNESS

The word "apocalypse" means "revelation." But it is a very special kind of revelation; it is the unveiling of God's secret plan for the end of time. The apocalyptic writings appear only in times of persecution and great stress, when the action of God is perceived as a dramatic intervention to set all the wrongs right, to rescue

God's oppressed people and to restore God's rule and sovereignty. Accordingly, the imagery of apocalyptic writings is often dramatic and violent. The destruction of the oppressors is described in great detail and, since this has not yet happened, everything is expressed in mysterious, symbolic language which is understood only by God's faithful and suffering people. The principal apocalyptic writings of the Bible are, in the Old Testament, the Book of Daniel and parts of Zechariah and, in the New Testament, the Book of Revelation and the "end of the world" chapters in the Synoptic gospels (Mark 13, Matthew 24-25 and Luke 21).

In order to appreciate the point of view of these important but often neglected apocalyptic writings, we must see how they presupposed and are related to the prophetic writings. The prophets were reformers in Israel. They attempted to call Israel back to the idealism of the time of Exodus when it was understood that the mission of God's people was to continue the wonder of Exodus by showing the whole world that loving service leading to freedom is the true purpose and calling of all God's human creatures. This ideal had been compromised as Israel, particularly under Solomon, had learned the pagan ways of power and domination. The prophets reminded Israel that God's promises can be realized in history but only where justice and mercy prevail.

As time passed, however, and Israel was herself reduced to suffering under the successive domination of the Assyrians, Babylonians, Persians and Greeks, it became more and more evident that God's kingdom could never be realized through the normal and ordinary processes of historical development. Divisions within Israel herself, as her people struggled to cope with this oppression, only added to the gloom. Paul Hanson sums it up admirably:

> The dawn of apocalyptic . . . follows upon the loss of this reasonable optimism of prophecy. Failure of the glorious promises of Second Isaiah to find fulfillment in the post-exilic community, disintegration of the sense of nationhood in the face of a schism rending the fabric of the people, oppression at the hands of fellow-Jews . . . such disappointments as these broke the optimism

> of prophetic eschatology with its belief that fulfillment
> of the vision of Yahweh's restoration of his people could
> occur within the context of this world (*The Dawn of
> Apocalyptic,* pp. 25-26).

The operative phrase here is "within the context of this world." Both prophetic and apocalyptic writers looked for realization of God's gracious plan for the world but it had now become clear to the apocalyptic visionaries that only dramatic, other-worldly intervention could bring that about. Accordingly, they looked for salvation from outside of history in a history-ending climactic victory of divine power.

The impact of this apocalyptic point of view on the message of Jesus has only recently been adequately noted. Jesus spoke constantly about the "kingdom of God"; he announced its imminent arrival and he told many parables to illustrate its nature. Most of his disciples misunderstood these words as they awaited a victory over the Roman oppressors and the restoration of David's political kingdom. It became clear, however, as Jesus moved toward his Passion that there would be no such restoration of this-worldly glories. Rather, the resurrection of Jesus marked a truly other-worldly intervention, a truly apocalyptic event, as the tables were suddenly and dramatically turned and the apparently defeated Messianic "pretender" was revealed to be not only Messiah but, almost incredibly, the very Son of God. The Resurrection of Jesus becomes, therefore, the ultimate apocalyptic event.

It must be noted, however, that the apocalyptic writers never dreamed that their predictions would be fulfilled in this manner. They pictured a violent and spectacular display that would end history and bring immediate and final judgment. But there was really no spectacular display in the last days of Jesus and what happened then in Jerusalem scarcely caused a ripple in the great Roman Empire. It was, of course, a tremendous event that would forever change the course of history, but it was at that time primarily a hidden, spiritual happening. Moreover, the

Resurrection of Jesus did not signal the end of history. It merely ushered in the "last days" in the sense that all history after Jesus exists on the threshold of eternity and each successive generation of believers must discover the meaning of Jesus in its own allotted time. Thus, the community of faith looks back at the end of the world represented by the death and resurrection of Jesus and, at the same time, prepares for the end of its own world as it strives to understand and embrace the redemption that Jesus brought to every phase of history.

As we strive to discover the full meaning of what Jesus did in our honest engagement with the present moment and in our yearnings for the future, we find ourselves, first of all, striving for the prophetic hope of salvation expressed in the fabric of human society and in the evolution of human history. In the measure that we can respond to the challenge of Jesus, we use our resources and our wits in a resolute search for justice and harmony and peace in this world — in families and communities and nations. But we grow old and feeble; we are forced to pass the flag to younger hands. At this critical moment, I think, we must acquire an apocalyptic consciousness; we must be willing to let go and to accept the fact of work unfinished as we lay aside our plans and prepare, calmly and cheerfully, for the end of our world. This is not at all mere stoic acceptance of the inevitable, nor is it even resignation to some higher power. Hopefully, it will be a positive welcoming of the mysterious but essentially good and trustworthy coming of the Lord. As in all apocalyptic events, the initial experience will be that of falling stars and darkness at noon as the familiar and hitherto reliable points of reference in our lives become more and more unstable. Paul Minear has pointed out (*New Testament Apocalyptic,* pp. 54-55) that, in the account of Genesis, the sun and moon and stars, created on the fourth day, were understood more as timepieces than as sources of light. When we grow old and have trouble remembering which meal comes next we will be experiencing the falling of the stars and the fading of the sun and moon! This kind of security is dispensable. It is the light of the first day of creation, supplied by faith and love, that will see us through when all else fails us.

In this way, our lives can become truly part of the experience of Jesus. For he did not teach escape from history. He "was born of the Virgin Mary, suffered under Pontius Pilate, died and was buried": he took history seriously. In the years of our strength we must also be engaged in history and strive to redeem the times. But neither did Jesus cling desperately to life. When he heard the Father's call, he let go of everything as he embraced God's will and entered the dark and chaotic experience of passion and death, fully confident that God's wonderful apocalyptic victory was just beyond the darkness. The Resurrection of Jesus stands as dramatic proof that all who embrace God's will as Jesus did will join him also in that victory.

THE SUFFERING OF ALONENESS

A great deal has been spoken and written about the virtues and importance of togetherness. Too little has been said about the reality and opportunity of aloneness. If togetherness means a sensitivity to the presence and value of other human beings, it is of course an ideal to be cherished and pursued. For no one, or at least no Christian, would defend the life of a loner or even a churlish hermit. But this pursuit of togetherness can obscure a very important reality, namely, the fact of a personal, private sanctuary in every human being. This sanctuary can be ignored but it will not go away. Nor can it be opened to all in some misguided search for absolute community. It is the center of one's being and ultimately it can be opened only to God. To surrender it to anyone but God is to become a slave; to surrender it to God is to be free forever.

Henri Nouwen has made an important distinction between loneliness and solitude (*Reaching Out*, pp. 22-23). Loneliness is the condition of one who feels abandoned; it is a sad and destructive state which should be avoided or relieved at all cost. It is part of our bondage. But solitude or aloneness is a normal and very healthy condition. It is the experience of a subtle, aching void which can be filled only by the Creator. Union with God in this life begins to fill this void and to ease this aching but full and final satisfaction and completion is reserved until one has left this earthly pilgrimage and rests at last in the bosom of the Father. There is a great temptation to try to fill this void with creatures but this always leads to disappointment; no one can take the place of God. Moreover, the creature who is asked to do so will sense that impossibility and will ultimately reject that burden. The only solution is to seek God fervently in this life, to love all creatures in a way that is in harmony with love of God and to suffer aloneness until the happy day of homecoming.

In the Passion of Jesus, we see him moving relentlessly toward ever greater isolation. He was certainly aware of the hostility of the Jewish leaders and he must have sensed the conspiracy that opens the Passion Narrative: ". . . and the chief priests and the doctors of the law were trying to devise some cunning plan to seize him and put him to death" (Mark 14:1). The leaders of the people he loved were plotting to kill him! Later on, in the garden of Gethsemane, his disciples abandoned him in the face of the mob that had come to seize him: "Then the disciples all deserted him and ran away"(Mark 14:50). Jesus was left alone, surrounded only by those who misunderstood and hated him. He met prejudice and rancor when facing the Sanhedrin and contempt before Pilate. Finally, he died alone, except for some women afar off (Mark 15:40). In Mark's version, even the repentant thief is absent, so that the aloneness of Jesus may appear in all its starkness.

In the days when I was master of novices in our monastery, I paid particular attention to signs of anti-social tendencies among the novices. In a Benedictine community it is essential that the monk be able to move easily among his confreres and to enjoy their company. But it is also important that he be able to live peacefully in his room. I would notice that some novices left their doors open all the time, apparently hoping that some passerby would come in to relieve their burdensome aloneness. I reminded them of the value of being alone at times, for serious study or reading or for private prayer. The ideal then is a balance between solitude and sociability.

I have often wondered too whether marriages might not be more successful if it were understood that no human being, including one's marriage partner, can take away the radical aloneness that is part of being human, a pilgrim away from home. If one expects marriage to remove even this experience of aloneness, there is a danger that one's partner will be blamed when that does not happen. This would be true especially where the marriage partners do not enjoy a good and rewarding relationship with God. Therefore, whatever our state of life may be, we must be prepared to join Jesus in this aloneness of his Passion and to cope, as he did, with rejection and misunderstanding by turning more and more to our Creator in whom alone we can find perfect rest and happiness. It should be noted, of course, that this recourse to God must not be used as an excuse for fleeing from the difficulties of human companionship. Rather, it is a realistic recognition of the limitations on what can be expected of human relationships. We need people and we need God. Jesus loved people but he did not ask them to fill the void that only God can fill.

PETER'S DENIAL OF JESUS

It is a little surprising that Peter's denial of his Master should be given so much attention in the Passion Narrative. Human sinfulness after all is not all that uncommon or even interesting. The fact that Peter's sin is described in such detail should alert us to a deeper, symbolic meaning that transcends the merely private elements of that episode. We recall that Peter had promised, in the strongest terms, that he would never abandon Jesus: "Peter answered, 'Everyone else may fall away, but I will not' " (14:29). When Jesus warned him that this night would cause even the strongest to fail, Peter ". . . insisted and repeated, 'Even if I must die with you, I will never disown you' " (14:31). I think that Jesus must have been very pleased to hear Peter say this even though he knew that the promise was beyond Peter's ability. Generosity is always beautiful, even when it is unrealistic!

Later, when Jesus was held captive in the high priest's residence, Peter, having found his way there, was questioned about his relationship to the Master. The maidservant noticed his uneasiness and asked whether he was not perhaps an associate of the prisoner. "But he denied it: 'I know nothing,' he said; 'I do not understand what you mean' "(14:68). But this evasive answer did not help. The noose tightened when "the bystanders said to Peter, 'Surely you are one of them. You must be; you are a Galilean' " (14:70), for they had detected his Galilean accent. "At this he broke out into curses, and with an oath he said, 'I do not know this man you speak of' " (14:71). When we note the strong Semitic implications of the verb, to know, we see that this means really: "This man means nothing to me!" The denial of Jesus is thus absolute and unmistakable. This represented a complete collapse of Peter's defenses. Jesus meant everything to him yet he found himself so shaken by fear that he denied his own truth. He was thus totally exposed as weak and helpless.

"Then the cock crew a second time; and Peter remembered how Jesus had said to him, 'Before the cock crows twice you will disown me three times.' And he burst into tears" (14:72). It is not necessary to believe that God had programmed a rooster to crow at this precise time! In the ancient world, the crowing of the cocks signaled the end of night and the beginning of a new day. When Jesus said that Peter would deny him three times (that is, unmistakably) before the cock crowed twice, he was simply saying that this would happen before the night was out. But, the crowing of the cock is emphasized for another reason as well. The cock, announcing dawn, was in a sense the alarm clock of those days, awakening people from the half-life of sleep to full reality. When Peter denied his Master, he too was "awakened" to the realization of his own weakness and limitations. He had made that brash promise under the illusion of invincibility. Now he had discovered how weak and frail he really was. His bitter weeping showed that he accepted this and deeply regretted what he had done. In this way, he let go of a certain falsehood or self-delusion and opened himself to divine grace and forgiveness. The cock-crow, therefore, signalled Peter's awakening from the half-life of illusion to the full awareness of truth about himself. On the basis of that truth, God was then able to work mightily through him in the years that followed as he became the rallying point for the infant church.

It is instructive to compare the denial of Peter to that of another apostle, Judas Iscariot. At first glance, one might think that Peter's sin was more grievous since he had explicitly promised to be faithful. When one considers the gospel portrait of Judas, however, it becomes clear that he would never have made the wild promise that Peter made for he was a cautious, calculating person. Peter's generosity and personal devotion may have led him to make an excessive promise but it also enabled him to repent and to become an even more perfect disciple. Judas' cautious and rational approach seemed at first to be wise and prudent but in the long run it brought only despair and suicide. The lesson is that we must be generous with God and people, saving our rational tendencies for dealing with projects and things!

JESUS ON TRIAL

After his arrest in the garden of Gethsemane, Jesus was brought for trial before the Jewish religious council, called the Sanhedrin. The gospel accounts vary but it seems that there was a preliminary hearing in the evening in the presence of the retired high priest, Annas, and then an official trial the following morning before Caiaphas. The charges brought against Jesus in this religious court were concerned with his alleged disrespect for the temple and his Messianic claims. As a matter of fact, they found him intolerable primarily because he was influential and uncontrollable. There is little doubt that Jesus did violate the rigid Sabbath laws but he did so to expose a legalism that had turned the Mosaic law of freedom into a source of guilt and scrupulosity. Moreover, he presented in his miracles clear credentials to support his prophetic activity by which he challenged a conservative and self-serving religious establishment.

When Caiaphas finally asked him: "Are you the Messiah, the Son of the Blessed one?" (14:61), he was asking whether he still claimed to be Messiah, even now that he stood bound and on trial. Jesus replied in the affirmative and reasserted his confidence in God's ultimate victory through him. The high priest considered this blasphemous because it would be offensive toward God to claim that he would send such a Messiah. Caiaphas then asked for and received the sentence of death prescribed for blasphemers. There is indeed a striking contrast between the robed and solemn judges on the one hand and the isolated, forlorn captive on the other. But Jesus did not waver. He let go of the illusion of apparent justice and clung resolutely to the justice of his own conscience. His lonely figure before the impressive membership of the Sanhedrin remains a perennial witness to the fact that justice and morality cannot always be assessed simply by majority vote or by the opinion of robed judges.

Though the Jewish council could try and condemn a defendant to death on religious charges, they could not carry out the sentence since the Roman civil authorities reserved execution to themselves. Thus, the Jewish authorities had to swallow their pride and go to Pilate, the Roman procurator, to seek this outcome. They realized that Pilate would not listen to religious charges and so they accused Jesus of sedition. This is ironic, of course, since they would have liked nothing better than to see the Romans expelled. Pilate saw through their subterfuge but realized that they could be troublesome if they incited the populace to riot and could thereby endanger his reputation in Rome where public order was given highest priority. When he heard that a crowd had gathered to make the customary request for release of a prisoner on the occasion of the Passover feast, he could not resist the temptation to torment the Jewish delegation by offering to release Jesus. However, they easily prompted the suspicious crowd to ask instead for Barabbas. Pilate agreed, not because he thought that Jesus was guilty, but simply because it was the expedient and pragmatic thing to do.

Since it was humiliating and distasteful for the Jewish authorities to have to appear before Pilate, one must wonder why they did not simply hire an assassin to kill Jesus. The answer seems to lie in the fact that they considered themselves law-abiding persons and had therefore to seek a legal solution to their problem. I heard once that a reporter was interviewing a notorious criminal and, to put him at his ease, offered him a cigarette. He refused immediately with the observation that smoking was not permitted in that place! Sometimes people who are very scrupulous about legal niceties have no problem at all about grievous moral offense. We must be concerned first of all with people and their rights; legal niceties and juridical appearances are completely secondary.

One cannot but be impressed by the contrast here again between the virtually silent, serene Jesus and the noise, distrust and animosity all around him. Pilate, the Jewish authorities and the crowd all had their special agendas, and they strove to steer the course of events to serve those purposes. Only Jesus was truly concerned with God's agenda and God's purposes; only he was in touch with what was rather than with what might be; only he put aside the illusion of control or manipulation and accepted the reality of life as given by God and made the most of it. Such contact with, and acceptance of, reality provides a sense of harmony and peace that stands in sharp contrast to the confusion and uncertainty that are so common in our experience. Peace can be found only in making the most of the life that we have; it is not found in day-dreams. The Passion of Jesus reminds us of the pain of such honesty but it is the only road to Resurrection.

THE CRUCIFIXION

The crucifixion of Jesus is never actually described in the gospels. Mark's version is typical: "Then they took him out to crucify him" (15:21). In all likelihood, this reticence is due to the authors' wish to emphasize, not the terrible suffering of Jesus, but the love that accepted this suffering and made it the perfect expression of sacrifice. The crucifixion was really a process. It began with the scourging by which the skin of the victim was broken by the blows of the scourge so that profuse bleeding would result. This was intended to weaken the victim so that the crucifixion itself would not be too prolonged. Since death by crucifixion was caused by asphyxiation when the knees buckled and the diaphragm was pulled up into the chest cavity, weakness was a major element in shortening the process (and thus shortening the soldiers' work). A major element in this process was the ridicule and humiliation of the victim which, in the case of Jesus, was especially degrading, first on the part of the Roman soldiers and later from the chief priests, the scribes and the passers-by. " 'Aha,' they cried, wagging their heads, 'you would pull the temple down, would you, and build it in three days? Come down from the cross and save yourself!'"(15:29-30).

Thus, Jesus was surrounded by misunderstanding and hostility on the part of those for whom he was dying and whom he truly loved. Just before the end, he cried out in the opening words of Psalm 22: "My God, my God, why hast thou forsaken me?", thus identifying himself with all those who have suffered unjustly and whose sacrifice has risen like precious incense before God. Finally, as he breathed his last, the centurion noted the extraordinary self-possession, love and compassion of Jesus, in contrast to others in whom he saw only resentment and despair, and exclaimed: " 'Truly this man was a son of God.' "(15:39).

It is important that we do not misunderstand and even trivialize the meaning of Jesus' death on the cross. This story is not given to us so that we may examine and savor every detail in a manner that is melodramatic or even morbid. Nor is it intended to provide an occasion for an unbridled self-recrimination or accusations of guilt. In fact, the crucifixion and the whole Passion Narrative are not primarily about how much Jesus suffered; they are about how much he loved! It is not a frightful story about thorns and nails and blood but a beautiful, comforting story about wonderful and unremitting love.

This primary meaning of the Passion story is clearly and unmistakably expressed in that somewhat mysterious episode that is described at the beginning of the Passion Narratives of Mark and Matthew, namely, the anointing of Jesus by an anonymous woman. It is generally agreed that this little story is inserted into the Passion story and interrupts it. Yet the reader is warned not to overlook it or to minimize its importance, for Jesus said: "I tell you this: wherever in all the world the Gospel is proclaimed, what she has done will be told as her memorial" (Mark 14:9). This strong statement is a kind of rubric that alerts us to some special significance of this story for the meaning of the entire Passion Narrative.

> Jesus was at Bethany, in the house of Simon the leper. As he sat at table, a woman came in carrying a small bottle of very costly perfume, oil of pure nard. She broke it open and poured the oil over his head (Mark 14:3).

There is something very spontaneous, almost impulsive, about this act. It is as if she had been waiting for just the right moment and, having found it, made the most of it. We should note in particular the absolute and generous nature of her gesture; it is total, final and irreversible. "Some of those present said to one another angrily, 'Why this waste? The perfume might have been sold for thirty pounds [literally, three hundred denarii] and the money given to the poor'; and they turned upon her with fury" (14:4-5). We cannot fail to be struck by the intensity of the reaction to her generous initiative. The bystanders were scandalized and offended by what they perceived to be a wasteful and extravagant action. They noted the great value of the ointment and claimed to be concerned about the loss to the poor for whom this might have been expended more wisely. We can easily appreciate their point of view. There had better be a very good reason for such an apparently foolish act.

> But Jesus said, 'Let her alone. Why must you make
> trouble for her? It is a fine thing she has done for me. You
> have the poor among you always, and you can help them
> whenever you like; but you will not always have me. She
> has done what lay in her power; she is beforehand with
> anointing my body for burial' (14:6-8).

Jesus rejected their protests out of hand. What she had done was
not wasteful and extravagant and foolish; it was not reprehensible at
all. On the contrary, what she had done was fine and beautiful and
praiseworthy! But the explanation of Jesus that follows is somewhat
obscure and has often been misunderstood. Most emphatically,
he was not saying that the fact of poverty should be accepted as
inevitable. It is a perversion to use this statement as an excuse for
neglecting the poor. Rather, Jesus was drawing their attention to his
own condition on the eve of his death. The bystanders pretended
to be worried about the poor but here was one right before them
who was desperate for comfort since no one is so poor as he who is
about to die. Only this woman had sensed his need and did what
was in her power to alleviate it. They talked about poverty; she
did something about it. Because she was helping one who was
on the verge of death, the anointing can truly be understood as
a preparation for burial.

This unmistakable reference to the death of Jesus relates this
episode to the Passion Narrative. It becomes a kind of keynote
or key signature that tells us how to read the beautiful music of
the Passion story. Far from being an interruption of that story, it
is essential to it because it tells us what to look for in it. For the
Passion Narrative is really the story of how Jesus showed himself
to be the ultimately sensitive one who noted our extreme poverty
and broke the "alabaster cruet" of his own body and poured out
the precious "ointment" of his life-blood to comfort and relieve all
of us who are about to die! That appears to be a very foolish and
wasteful thing to do and the followers of Jesus will be ridiculed if
they imitate him by dedicating their lives to loving service. But in

fact it is a fine and beautiful thing to do. It is the very language of true love which has its own special kind of logic that is quite different from the pragmatic logic of selfishness. It is like giving cut flowers; they are so perishable that giving them seems a bit wasteful. However, the one who receives them knows what they mean and sees how they express the foolish wisdom of love and is deeply affected by that message.

There is much suffering in the Passion of Jesus; but most of all there is loving. Instead of feeling sorry for Jesus in his suffering, we should strive to imitate him in his loving. That will bring us suffering too but it will be the "good" suffering that is sacrifice and that leads to freedom and glory. We should be very careful about assuming that our suffering is the same as that of Jesus. His suffering came from his love; ours may often come from frustration and disappointment because we don't get our own way. Such suffering is useless for salvation. To join Jesus in his Passion we must let go of selfish plans and learn to love and sacrifice and thus prepare for our union with him in Resurrection victory.

HELLO AND GOODBYE

It is impossible to make the biblical journey of faith without dealing with the problem of saying Goodbye. Every step forward means a step away from something. Sometimes the present is so painful that it is easy to leave it but more frequently we hesitate to greet the future because we want to cling to what we have. On the all important personal level, the threat of Goodbye is always present. It is almost a truism that those who dare to love will soon learn also how to grieve. In fact we may be tempted, especially in later years, to limit our Hellos because we feel that we cannot run the risk of even more Goodbyes. This may be what is meant in a line of that beautiful and poignant song, "Leaving on a Jet Plane": "I hate to wake you up to say Goodbye." Many of these folk songs, being close to human experience, are full of references to the impermanence of human existence. It would be a serious mistake, however, to withdraw from life in order to avoid Goodbyes or to stop "waking" people by love for fear of eventual separation.

Jesus had much to say about this dilemma. He said Hello to everyone and everything. When the disciples tried to protect him by chasing away the children he protested and insisted that they be allowed to approach him. He said Hello to publicans and sinners as well as to the more respectable folk. But he also said Goodbye. He said Goodbye to life when he was in his prime and he said Goodbye to all his friends. He did so cheerfully, resolutely and without hesitation. He was able to do so, it seems, because he had discovered the secret of the Hello/Goodbye rhythm of life. The threat of Goodbye has power to frighten and paralyze us because it appears that, no matter how often we say Hello, it is Goodbye that conquers in the end; it appears that death has the last word. But that is only an appearance. The secret of Jesus and the secret of faith is the sure conviction that death is in turn conquered by life in the victory of Resurrection. That means that Hello has the last word; it is a resounding Hello that echoes for all eternity! If we truly believe, then we will, like Jesus, be able to say Hello to all of life and, when the time comes, to say Goodbye also, because we will trust the Father's love and the power of the Resurrection and the ultimate victory of Hello. This will enable us to make decisions and commitments that may close as well as open doors, that include Goodbyes as well as Hellos, because we will know instinctively that the one who says Hello in love and Goodbye in love will find at the end that all the Hellos have been saved in that one last unconquerable Hello of Resurrection. The Passion of Jesus was painful because it was letting go, it was saying Goodbye, it was loving to the end; but it was a joy too because it was persevering in love and thus preparing for Resurrection. It was total Goodbye in trust to permit total Hello in glory.

9

The Resurrection As Homecoming

When I was a seminary student in the late 1940s, the Resurrection of Jesus was presented as that great miracle by which he demonstrated, once and for all, his truly divine nature. It was seen, therefore, as just another element in the apologetic enterprise to which so much of theology was then devoted. It was like a breath of fresh air when F. X. Durwell"s book, *The Resurrection,* appeared in 1960. He put aside apologetic concerns and showed that the Resurrection was simply the last climactic step in a wonderful process of salvation. It did, of course, reveal clearly the divinity of Jesus, but most of all it showed the Father welcoming home his Son after a long and difficult journey. The Resurrection was a homecoming. It epitomized all the joy and relief and satisfaction that we associate with that happy experience in our own imperfect and limited lives. Resurrection is perfect, unqualified, eternal homecoming!

In the baptism, Jesus had stood with a penitent and expectant Israel pleading for the long-delayed Messianic salvation. God responded with the assurance that the time of redemption had come. In the strength of those comforting words, Jesus went forth and announced the imminence of God's kingdom. Later on, as he discovered that the coming of this kingdom would cost him suffering, ignominy and death, he again accepted the Father's will, now wrapped in mystery, and the Father affirmed him again in the stirring words from heaven at the transfiguration: "This is my Son, my Beloved; listen to him" (Mark 9:7). At the third and final critical turning-point of his ministry, we see Jesus accept the Father's will at Gethsemane. But we wait in vain, it seems, for the answering affirmation and reassurance of the Father. This puzzled me until one day it dawned on me that the Resurrection was that response. For there, in effect, the Father embraced his Son with the words: "Welcome home, my Son!" We cannot hear those words because they presuppose the final obedience of a death accepted trustingly from God but we are assured that, if we can be ready for the final gift, as Jesus was, we too will feel the embrace and hear those wonderful words.

THE EMPTY TOMB

The earliest account of the Resurrection of Jesus is that found in Mark's gospel and it is surprisingly indirect in its testimony. The original Resurrection story makes no mention of an appearance of the risen Jesus but shows us only the empty tomb. Appearances are noted only in a later ending to the gospel, 16:9-20, which is missing in many early manuscripts. This does not suggest at all that the appearances are untrustworthy; it merely reminds us that the defeat of death was noted before the victory of life.

Mark's account is remarkably straightforward. Some women went to the tomb early Sunday morning to provide the embalming service which they assumed had not been given and, as they wondered how they would roll back the large stone at the mouth of the cave-like tomb, they discovered, to their astonishment, that the stone was already removed. "They went into the tomb, where they saw a youth sitting on the right-hand side, wearing a white robe; and they were dumbfounded" (Mark 16:5). The white robe identified the young man as an angel. As such, he represented God and expressed a divine revelation of the meaning of this unexpected development: "But he said to them, 'Fear nothing; you are looking for Jesus of Nazareth, who was crucified. He has been raised again;

he is not here; look, there is the place where they laid him' " (Mark 16:6). The angel reassured them and eliminated certain possible explanations: the body has not been stolen and they have not found the wrong tomb. Jesus has been raised from the dead; the tomb could not hold him; he is victor over death! One must be precise here; Jesus did not "come back" from the dead. The daughter of Jairus (Mark 5:41-42) came back from the dead and died again later! Jesus went *beyond* death into a new kind of life that is radically different from the life he possessed before crucifixion. This was expressed aptly by the German theologian, Jürgen Moltmann, when he wrote:

> By 'resurrection' the earliest Christians did not mean a return of the dead Christ into mortal life or a restoration of the fallen creation. They meant, rather, the entrance of something completely unexpected, the inbreaking of a qualitatively new future and the appearance of a life which is no longer 'life toward death' but 'life out of death' (*Religion, Revolution and the Future*, p. 33).

In recent years, some scholars have questioned the bodily resuscitation of Jesus and have concluded that such language is simply a literary device to express the faith of the first Christians in the Resurrection of Jesus. Whatever one may think about this opinion it is important to note that they are not denying the Resurrection in its essential meaning as the victory of Jesus over sin and death. Rather, they are pointing out that the bodily resurrection of Jesus was simply a sign of that victory and hence not an essential part of it. However, many would contend that it was not a sign whose historical reality can be easily questioned. Rather, it would seem that the biblical authors are quite insistent on the importance of that sign. Vincent Taylor writes:

> In view of the intimate connexion between the body and the soul or spirit in Jewish thought there can be little doubt that, when in the earliest preaching it was affirmed that God raised up Jesus from the dead (Acts 2:24, 31f;

3:15, etc.), an empty tomb was implied, and, further, that
the same implication underlies the words of Saint Paul in
1 Cor 15:3-5 . . . (*The Gospel of Mark,* p.606).

In other words, the assumption is that a bodily resurrection was
intended by the biblical writers and the contrary must be clearly
demonstrated. In my opinion, that has not yet been done.

At the same time, we must not make the mistake of reducing
the Resurrection to a simple, controllable historical event. It was
a tremendous eschatological event — a kind of explosion on the
frontier between time and eternity. It was both historical and
metahistorical: in time and beyond time. Its deepest meaning can
be perceived only through the eyes of faith and, once perceived,
it reveals the meaning of human existence with a clarity that had
never existed before. The path of Jesus, a path of loving service,
is not the folly that it seems to be, for it leads to eternal life. And
the path of selfish pursuits is not the wisdom it seems to be, for it
leads to defeat and frustration.

THE RESURRECTION APPEARANCES

There were several appearances after the Resurrection. Three
of them are mentioned more than once: the appearance to Mary
Magdalene (Mark 16:6, Matt 28:9 and John 20:14-18); to the
Eleven (Mark 16:14, Matt 28:16-20 in Galilee, Luke 24:36-51)
in Jerusalem; and to two disciples on the way to Emmaus (Luke
24:13-32, Mark 16:12). These appearance stories represent different
traditions which are difficult if not impossible to reconcile. They
are very important, however, because they express in various ways
the discovery of Resurrection faith among the followers of Jesus.
As Raymond Brown puts it:

> In the genesis of resurrection faith it was the appearance
> of the glorified Lord that first brought his disciples to
> believe; and this belief, in turn, interpreted the empty

> tomb. Having seen the risen Jesus, they understood that
> the reason why the tomb was empty was because he had
> been raised from the dead (*The Virginal Conception and
> the Bodily Resurrection of Jesus*, p.127).

The appearance and words of the angel would then be simply a way of providing the interpretation that came really from the appearances.

Since it is so difficult to reconcile the various traditions, it is not surprising that scholars should differ considerably in their attempts to reconstruct the sequence of events after the Resurrection. Raymond Brown offers a tentative reconstruction which can be summarized as follows: The disciples returned to Galilee and to their previous lives after the death of Jesus. Then, Jesus appeared to Peter and to the others in Galilee where "resurrection faith was born." These appearances implied a mission to proclaim the good news of Jesus' victory. Finally, the disciples went to Jerusalem for the feast of Pentecost with its "charismatic manifestation of the Spirit" and their apostolic work continued from there. (See: *The Virginal Conception and the Bodily Resurrection of Jesus*, pp. 108-111). It is important to note that, though we yearn for a logical reconstruction, this was apparently of little concern to the authors of the gospels. Their primary interest lay in the meaning of the appearances as a whole rather than in their sequence or reconciliation with one another.

The words of Jesus are crucial to the meaning of the appearances. Time and again it is reported that those who saw Jesus were astonished, filled with awe and fear. "Startled and terrified, they thought they were seeing a ghost" (Luke 24:37). Jesus hastened to reassure them.

> But he said, 'Why are you so perturbed? Why do questionings
> arise in your minds? Look at my hands and feet. It is I myself.
> Touch me and see; no ghost has flesh and bones as you can
> see that I have.' They were still unconvinced, still wondering,
> for it seemed too good to be true. So he asked them, 'Have
> you anything here to eat?' They offered him a piece of fish

they had cooked, which he took and ate before their eyes
(Luke 24:38-43).

The words to notice in this passage are: ". . . it seemed too
good to be true." They desperately wanted to believe that Jesus
was alive and present but, like most human beings, they had
steeled themselves for disappointment. Jesus told them that, on this
occasion, on this most important occasion, they may trust their
wildest dreams. Tragedy has been turned to triumph; tragedy has
suddenly become manageable!

This presence of Jesus, though very real, is not the presence that
they knew before the crucifixion. Jesus has not simply come back
to life; rather, he has appeared, truly but transformed, from that
new life. This is made abundantly clear in the exchange between
Jesus and Mary Magdalene. When she saw Jesus and thought he
was the gardener he called her by name and she recognized him.
What followed was surprising: "Jesus said, 'Do not cling to me
[literally, touch me no more], for I have not yet ascended to the
Father'"(John 20:17). We must assume that Mary embraced Jesus
in some fashion with the implication: "Thank God you're back."
But Jesus reminded her that he had not really come back to her;
rather he had come to urge her and all of us to come soon and
without hesitation to the place where he waits for us with the
Father. He was present to her, therefore, as one from another world,
as one who revealed some of the joy of that world as he called
her (and calls us) to join him there. This does not mean that the
presence of Jesus in the appearances was ethereal or somehow
unreal. On the contrary, it was a presence more real and experienced
than any merely physical presence, but it was different and it
suggested an incompleteness, a need to strive toward a more perfect
and final presence.

The effect of the appearances of Jesus on his disciples is summed
up in that richly significant word Peace (Hebrew: Shalom).

Late that Sunday evening, when the disciples were together
behind locked doors, for fear of the Jews, Jesus came and

> stood among them. 'Peace be with you!' he said, and then
> showed them his hands and his side. So when the disciples
> saw the Lord, they were filled with joy (John 20:19-20).

This peace is not just the absence of war or dissension. It has profound positive implications suggesting a state of supreme well-being, the sense of being fully accepted, of being in exactly the right place at exactly the right time. There is profound contentment but not smugness. This kind of peace can be given only by God since it reflects the deep sense of freedom and confidence that comes from knowing and feeling the love of God.

This wonderful experience of salvation is not for private enjoyment, however; the discovery of Jesus' victory demands proclamation. If it is too good to be true, it is also too good to keep to oneself. "Jesus repeated, 'Peace be with you!', and said, 'As the Father sent me, so I send you' " (John 20:21). In John's gospel, Jesus speaks constantly about his mission from the Father. His challenging message of loving service is trustworthy because it has come from the Father. Now that the wisdom of that ideal has been forever confirmed by his victory over death, he sends the disciples to proclaim and to live that truth so that all may share in his victory. The same urgency is found in the conclusion of Matthew's gospel:

> (Jesus) said, 'Full authority in heaven and on earth has been
> committed to me. Go forth therefore and make all nations
> my disciples; baptize men [and women] everywhere in the
> name of the Father and the Son and the Holy Spirit, and
> teach them to observe all that I have commanded you.
> And be assured, I am with you always, to the end of time'
> (28:18-20; see also Mark 16:15).

Jesus simply pointed out what was already inherent in the very experience of Resurrection faith; if it is real it must be proclaimed to others! Moreover, the presence of that faith will imply the comforting presence of Jesus himself for all ages. Jesus thus reaffirmed definitively the ancient covenant formula: "I will become your God and you shall be my people" (Lev 26:12), that is, I shall be with you always to comfort and protect you and you shall show yourself my people by gladly entertaining my presence in sincere worship and loving care of others.

When the risen Lord met those two disciples on the way to Emmaus, he chided them because they did not understand the Scriptures.

> 'How dull you are! How slow to believe all that the prophets said! Was the Messiah not bound to suffer thus before entering upon his glory?' Then he began with Moses and all the prophets, and explained to them the passages which referred to himself in every part of the scriptures (Luke 24:25-27).

The disciples certainly were quite familiar with the Hebrew scriptures. Their mistake was to assume that they understood them, to assume that their mystery had been exhausted. The scriptures had become for them like an old friend who had told all his stories and had no surprises left. But Jesus took them on a brief tour of those scriptures and showed them how much mystery was still there and how that mystery contained the wonderful meaning that they only now comprehended. What had seemed old and exhausted was suddenly full of vitality and meaning. "They said to one another, 'Did we not feel our hearts on fire as he talked with us on the road and explained the scriptures to us?' " (Luke 24:32). This stirring experience remains a possibility for all of us. Resurrection faith sensitizes us to the meaning hidden in creation, in people and, especially, in God. The dark cloud is illuminated and our hearts are on fire!

Later on, Luke describes how Jesus appeared to the apostles and others at Jerusalem and explained more fully this deeper meaning of the scriptures.

> And he said to them, 'This is what I meant by saying, while I was still with you, that everything written about me in the Law of Moses and in the prophets and psalms

> was bound to be fulfilled'. Then he opened their minds
> to understand the scriptures. 'This,' he said, 'is what
> is written: that the Messiah is to suffer death and to
> rise from the dead on the third day, and that in his
> name repentance bringing the forgiveness of sins is to be
> proclaimed to all nations. Begin from Jerusalem; it is you
> who are the witnesses to it all' (Luke 24:44-48).

The suffering and death of a very promising but merely human and political Messiah to make room for God's divine and death-defeating Messiah was not just a private affair involving Jesus. It was a paradigm and model for the painful but necessary death of human plans and human understandings to make room for God's far better design and ultimate wisdom. The Resurrection shows how wise it is to be diffident about human plans and to embrace God's ways.

Luke then provides a concrete example of what embracing God's plan can mean. The earliest Christian communities were made up almost exclusively of Jews who had accepted Jesus and his message as the fulfillment of the promises made to Israel. They continued to observe Jewish laws and customs while celebrating the Eucharist in their homes (Acts 2:46). It is almost impossible for us to realize how difficult it was for these Jewish Christians to deal with the issue of converts from paganism. They still felt the deep and ancient Jewish antagonism toward the Gentiles but it was becoming more and more obvious that God had chosen the Gentiles too, as Peter learned when he saw the Holy Spirit come down upon Cornelius and his family (Acts 10:44-45).

Since Luke himself was a convert from paganism he could readily appreciate the importance of this opening up of the infant church to the whole human race. As the author of Acts, he documented this wonderful development. This became for him a sign and warrant of Resurrection faith. Small wonder then that he should have shown Jesus declaring the centrality of his death and resurrection and then adding immediately: "and that in his name repentance bringing the forgiveness of sins is to be proclaimed to all nations" (Luke 24:47). This proclamation is to go out from

Jerusalem for, just as in Luke's gospel everything flows toward Jerusalem, so also in the Acts everything flows out of Jerusalem as the Good News is announced to the whole world. To possess authentic Resurrection faith means therefore to be endlessly open to God's mysterious and wonderful ways. What life brings is not to be fought and resisted as we struggle to have it our way; rather, the events of life, including death itself, are to be welcomed as moments of grace and opportunities for trust and love. Instead of trying desperately to create a safe little world where we can live undisturbed (and miss life!), we should be striving constantly to welcome the "Gentiles" and other "strangers" and thereby to make room for God's wonderful surprises.

In the second ending of Mark's gospel (16:12-20), the resurrection appearance of Jesus brings a promise of most unusual results among the community of believers. Jesus told the disciples,

> Faith will bring with it these miracles: believers will cast out devils in my name and speak in strange tongues; if they handle snakes or drink any deadly poison, they will come to no harm; and the sick on whom they lay their hands will recover (Mark 16:17-18).

The devils who will be cast out are not the kind featured in melodramatic stories of exorcism but the everyday and more dangerous demons of dissension and distrust and hatred. Everywhere in Scripture the demons are portrayed as agents of chaos who are in constant conflict with the divine work of creation with its light and peace and order. The power of faith will continue therefore the beautiful work of creation as God's power works through the believer to conquer chaos and bring light and harmony and peace. Faith will also overcome the chaos symbolized by divergent tongues or languages. Babel will be replaced with Pentecost. The men of Babel resisted God's will and feared his call with the result that they could no longer live in harmony; the men of Pentecost welcome God's call to be scattered in loving service with the result that they, though belonging to many nations, speak the one language of the Spirit.

The venomous serpents and poisonous drink of this text are to be understood symbolically. The life of faith is a journey through the wilderness of God's mystery. Two classic dangers for the traveler in the ancient world were poisonous serpents hiding along the unfamiliar path and the poison lurking in unknown and contaminated wells. For the believer these are the poisons of despair and cynicism. Only strong and vital faith can give one immunity from their ravages. Finally, the believer will bring a healing touch to every situation. This may occasionally involve physical healing but far more often it will entail the more important healing of anger, resentment, guilt and the like. Thus, we have the promise of Jesus himself that his resurrection will release a tremendous power for good which will be administered through those who believe for the benefit of all.

The kind of faith that will produce such benefits is not just an affirmation of the fact of Jesus' resurrection. It must be a personal experience of the power of that victory. Such an experience will show that the resurrection was not only the event that made wonderful sense out of all that had happened to Jesus but that it is the event which continues to reveal the meaning of the whole Bible . . . and therefore the meaning of our lives. This is aptly expressed in the words of Arthur Michael Ramsey:

> Throughout the Old Testament, there had been the strain of a tension which, it seemed, could never be resolved. On the one hand there was the faith of Israel in God's sovereignty and righteousness and faithfulness to his people. On the other hand there were the sufferings of the righteous and the cries of the afflicted. The tension ran through the history of Israel, and it sometimes strained the faith of Israel nearly to the point of breaking. But, now that the Christ has himself suffered and been raised from death, the tension within the Scriptures has been resolved and the unity of the Scriptures has been disclosed. For it is perceived that the sufferings of the Servant of the Lord do not contradict the sovereign power of God; rather are these sufferings the means whereby God has wrought mightily in

His purpose to deliver mankind (*The Resurrection of Christ,* p. 26).

CONTEMPLATIVE PRAYER

It is all well enough to read and study the biblical accounts of the glorious resurrection of Jesus and of his appearances to his overjoyed disciples but we remain in our own bondage of fear and uncertainty and weakness. It does help to gaze longingly at the victory and homecoming of Jesus but we need some sure way to bridge the tremendous gap between our present experience and that final liberation. Jesus has promised to be with us until the end and he has given us his Spirit to guide and encourage us on the difficult journey of faith. There are many ways by which we can draw upon the strength of that divine presence but one that is often overlooked is the very helpful way of quiet, contemplative prayer.

We should by all means engage in public and communal prayer, especially the formal, liturgical prayer of the Church, and many have benefited also from more informal, charismatic prayer. But we need also to engage in fervent and regular private, personal prayer. An ancient and truly effective form of personal prayer is the prayer of quiet. This simply means setting aside twenty minutes or half an hour once a day to sit quietly and be totally attentive to the Lord. Of course, there will be distractions but we must not be discouraged. The success of the prayer really does not consist in eliminating all distractions but rather in the loving effort to make the time available and to do one's best to be attentive. If thoughts of urgent needs come to mind, one simply lays them quietly before the Lord in the sure knowledge that nothing more practical can be done at that moment. Some recommend the use of a mantra, such as the name of Jesus, to recall one's attention gently to the presence of the Lord. If this helps, all well and good, but the most important consideration here is not technique but simple faithfulness to the practice of this prayer. If our human friends are pleased and honored when we make time for them in our busy schedules, we can assume that God is even more pleased and will use this opportunity to change us in the ways that seem best to him.

It will seem, of course, that this is all a waste of precious time that could be spent better in some good work. But then we should recall what was said when the woman anointed Jesus with precious ointment: "Why this waste? The perfume might have been sold . . . and the money given to the poor" (Mark 14:4-5)! To anoint Jesus with the gift of our precious time may seem wasteful but Jesus will say to us, as he did to that generous woman, "It is a fine thing she has done for me" (Mark 14:6). It is true that, by the standard of our noisy world, it will seem that nothing is being accomplished. However, God works in subtle and quiet ways to achieve his mighty purposes. If we are faithful to this prayer, we will notice that some very important things are happening.

We will gradually become more attuned to mystery in our lives and especially to the ultimate mystery in God. We will move from fearing mystery to embracing it. For it will become more and more evident that the richest source of goodness in our lives is not that small and shrinking part of life that can be understood and controlled but rather that enormous and growing part of life that is largely incomprehensible and well beyond our control. Thus we will be able to renounce finally the remnants of idolatry by which we try to remove the threat of the Unknown One by reducing him to our own finite measurements and will be able finally to rejoice in and give thanks for the fully sovereign, terribly mysterious and wonderfully gracious God of reality. As we move into this wilderness land of mystery, where trust counts for everything, we will dare to notice our own radical contingency, our "nothingness," because we will be now in the presence of the "allness" of God.

It is impossible to put limits on what might happen in such an encounter between a sincere and generous person and an all-loving God. The least that can happen is that one will be gradually changed. The Lord will truly speak in that silence and the one who hears him will become more confident, calmer, more able to be patient with others, more sensitive, more able to put aside illusions and face the truth, more able to cope with problems; he will be less angry and frustrated, less fearful, especially less fearful of death. But, most of all, one will be refreshed and strengthened for love and service. And all of this will help to bring about that painful conversion by which we participate in the Passion of Jesus and prepare for our own wonderful homecoming.

"THEN I SAW A NEW HEAVEN AND A NEW EARTH" (REVELATION 21:1)

Probably everyone will agree that the Book of Revelation is about a furious and decisive struggle between the forces of good and evil. There is less agreement about the identity of those forces. Those who make specific and literal applications to contemporary events are almost certainly misrepresenting the text. The struggle is essentially between those who trust in power and violence to achieve their ends and those who trust in the power of love and good will supported by the power of God. The former were the representatives of the Roman Empire at the time of the author but they have heirs in every generation, sometimes even within the churches. The latter were the politically and economically powerless Christians who were actively persecuted by the Roman authorities. Apparently, some Christians maintained that a compromise could be worked out but this is rejected out of hand by the author of Revelation. Christian faith requires that one make choices and live by them.

It is tempting, of course, to indulge one's own favorite prejudices in deciding who are good and approved by God. In fact, those approved by Revelation are the ones who make the basic choices required of Christians by Jesus himself. They are to be followers of the Lamb, who is the very symbol of the one who loved all and gave up his life for their salvation. To love in this way is so difficult that one is constantly tempted to substitute appearances for reality, to claim to be a follower of Jesus but to continue to live in a self-centered way. It is for this reason, no doubt, that Revelation condemns every form of deceit and calls for absolute sincerity and honesty. The final judgment will expose all the many forms of hypocrisy and reward genuine virtue. Those who have struggled to rid themselves of illusion and to embrace the painful but liberating truth will be vindicated by him who is all truth.

This does not mean that Christianity is only for heroes. God's love and grace are available to all. But we must realize that God loves us as we are and that his love can transform us only on condition that we are willing to be what we are, honestly and cheerfully, and then, with his help, to become what he wants us to be. This process of conversion is not easy but it is so much better than all the other options. Moreover, it gives meaning and purpose to our lives and leads us gradually to the moment when we will be ready to become part of the new heaven and the new earth.

> I heard a loud voice proclaiming from the throne: 'Now at last God has his dwelling among men! He will dwell among them and they shall be his people, and God himself will be with them. He will wipe every tear from their eyes; there shall be an end to death, and to mourning and crying and pain; for the old order has passed away!' (Rev 21:3-4).

When we hear that voice we will know the full meaning of Jesus' resurrection and we will also know that we have successfully completed the journey and have arrived at our true home.

BIBLIOGRAPHY

Benoit, Pierre: *The Passion and Resurrection of Jesus Christ* (Herder and Herder, NY, 1969).

Brown, Raymond: *The Community of the Beloved Disciple* (Paulist Press, NY, 1979).

Brown, Raymond: *The Gospel According to John,* AB, Two volumes (Doubleday, Garden City, NY, 1966, 1970).

Brown, Raymond: "The Pater Noster as an Eschatological Prayer" in *Theological Studies 22* (1961), 175-208.

Brown, Raymond: *The Virginal Conception and Bodily Resurrection of Jesus* (Paulist Press, NY, 1973).

Brueggemann, Walter: *David's Truth* (Fortress Press, Philadelphia, 1985).

Brueggemann, Walter: *The Prophetic Imagination* (Fortress Press, Philadelphia, 1978).

Brunner, Emil: *The Divine-Human Encounter* (Westminster Press, Philadelphia, 1943).

Buber, Martin: *On Judaism* (Schocken Books, NY, 1967).

Buber, Martin: *On the Bible* (Schocken Books, NY, 1968).

Durwell, F. X.: *The Resurrection* (Sheed and Ward, NY, 1960).

Eliot, T. S.: *Murder in the Cathedral* (Harcourt, Brace and Co., NY, 1935).

Fitzmyer, Joseph: *The Gospel According to Luke,* AB, Vol 1 (Doubleday, Garden City, NY, 1981).

Hammarskjöld, Dag: *Markings* (Alfred A. Knopf, NY, 1965).

Hanson, Paul: *The Dawn of Apocalyptic* (Fortress Press, Philadelphia, 1975).

Minear, Paul: *New Testament Apocalyptic* (Abingdon, Nashville, TN, 1981).

Moltmann, Jürgen: *Religion, Revolution and the Future* (Charles Scribner's Sons, NY, 1969).

Moltmann, Jürgen: *The Theology of Hope* (Harper and Row, NY, 1967).

Murray, John C.: *The Problern of God* (Yale University Press, New Haven, 1964).

Noth, Martin: *Exodus* (Old Testament Library) (Westminster Press, Philadelphia, 1962).

Nouwen, Henri J.M.: *Reaching Out* (Doubleday, Garden City, NY, 1975).

Ramsey, A. Michael: *The Glory of God and the Transfiguration of Christ* (Longmans, Green, London, 1949).

Ramsey, A. Michael: *The Resurrection of Christ* (Geoffrey Bles, London, 1945).

RB 1980, *The Rule of Saint Benedict,* ed., Timothy Fry (Liturgical Press, Collegeville, MN, 1981).

Richardson, Herbert: *Toward an American Theology* (Harper and Row, NY, 1967).

Sainte Thérèse. *Derniers Entretiens* (Editions du Cerf, Paris, 1971).

Index of Biblical References

OLD TESTAMENT
Genesis

1:1-2:4	19
1:2	28
1:3	30
1:27	112
1:28	15
1:31	15
2:2-3	15
2:5-25	19
11:4	68
11:9	68
12:1	67
12:4	67
13:16	67
18:1-15	67
18:10	68
18:11	67
21:5	67

Exodus

2:23	6
2:23-25	6
3:1	7
3:7-8	7
3:10	8
3:11	8
3:14	8, 77, 78, 100
4:10-14	8
4:31	9
5:1	61
12:7-11	57
12:11	59
16:2-4	97
19:4	11
20:2	12
20:2-17	12
20:3	13
20:4-5	13
20:7	14
20:8-11	14
20:12	16
20:13	17
20:14	17
20:15	17
20:16	18
20:17	18

Leviticus

26:12	11, 78, 160
26:13	22

Numbers

11:5	64
11:7-9	97
11:10-15	64
14:1	64
14:9	64

14:10	64	109	49
14:11	64	114:1	11
14:22-23	64	114:3-4	11
		114:7-8	11

Deuteronomy

4:7-8	44	**Proverbs**	
5:6-21	12	9:5	102
6:4-9	11		
24:17	52	**Ecclesiastes**	
24:17-18	45	11:1	94
26:5	24		
26:5-9	10	**Isaiah**	
		1:15-17	53
1 Samuel		42:1	29
9:2	41	55:10	102
13:3-14	41	64:1	28
15	41		
17:12-54	42	Jeremiah	
21:3-6	41	7:4	86
		7:11	87
2 Samuel			
6:14	42	**Zechariah**	
6:21	42	14:21	87
11	41		

NEW TESTAMENT

1 Kings		**Matthew**	
18:7-16	84	1	72
19:12	83	2	72
21:15	83	3:13-17	27
		3:14	28
Psalms		5:3-10	37
2:7	29	6:9	121, 123, 124
14:1	78	6:9-13	121
22:1	80, 149	6:10	124, 125
95:8-10	65	6:11	125

6:12	126	14:31	144
6:13	127	14:32	135
6:14-15	127	14:33	136
15:6	87	14:34	136
16:19	130	14:35-36	136
18:1-4	36	14:37	137
24	139	14:38	137
25	139	14:50	143
26:60-61	85	14:59	85
28:9	157	14:61	147
28:16-20	157	14:68	145
28:18-20	160	14:70	145
		14:71	145
Mark		14:72	145
1:9-11	27	15:21	148
1:10	28	15:29-30	149
1:11	29, 91	15:31-32	76
5:41-42	156	15:34	80
8:27-29	89	15:39	149
8:31-32	90	15:40	143
9:2	89, 136	16:5	155
9:3	91	16:6	155, 157
9:5	91	16:9-20	155
9:6	91	16:12	157
9:7	91, 155	16:12-20	163
9:41	84	16:14	157
11:15-18	86	16:15	160
13	139	16:17-18	163
14:1	135, 143		
14:3	150	**Luke**	
14:4-5	150, 166	1	72
14:6	166	1:38	72
14:6-8	151	1:48	72
14:9	150	2	72
14:29	144	2:35	73

2:49	73	3:19	31
4:1-2	73	6	99
6:20-23	37	6:1-15	99
9:51	70	6:9	99
11:1	120	6:11	100
11:2-4	121	6:12	100
12:16-21	72	6:16-21	100
14:33	71	6:18	100
15:1-2	70	6:19-21	100
15:7	71	6:20	100
16:19-31	72	6:27	101
21	139	6:29	101
24:13-32	157	6:30-35	101
24:16	69	6:35-50	102
24:21	69	6:47	101
24:25-27	161	6:48-50	101
24:27	69	6:51	102
24:29	69	6:51-58	99
24:31	69	6:53-54	102
24:32	161	6:55-56	103
24:36-51	157	6:58	103
24:37	158	8:44	76
24:28-43	158	8:58	129
24:44-48	161	14:16	130
24:47	162	14:26	74
		16:8-11	75
John		16:13-14	130
1:1	30	20:14-18	157
1:3	30	20:17	159
1:4	30	20:19-20	159
1:5	30	20:21	160
1:10-12	31		
1:14	31	**Acts of the Apostles**	
1:38	60	2:24	156
3:3-8	31	2:31f	156

2:46	162	**2 Corinthians**
3:15	156	4:10	94
10:44-45	162	4:16	94
		12:10	38
Romans		
3:20	44	**Galatians**
3:21-22	33	4:6	105
3:24	33, 34	
3:28	116	**Ephesians**
4:16	33	1:14	106
4:19-21	68	2:17-18	106
8:14-16	105	2:19	106
8:22-24	106	5:18-20	107
8:26-27	107	
8:38-39	103	**Hebrews**
		3:17-19	66
1 Corinthians		11:1	98
2:10	73	11:1-40	34
11:16-34	50	
11:17-34	103	**1 John**
12	109	3:16	46
12:4-6	113	4:11	46
12:7	115	
12:7-11	114	**Revelation**
12:14-20	110	21:1	167
12:21-26	110	21:3-4	168
12:31	116	
13:1	116	
13:4	117, 118	
13:5	118, 119	
13:6	119	
13:7	119	
15:3-5	157	

Index of Authors

Augustine, Saint   60

Benedict, Saint   95
Benoit, Pierre   137
Brown, Raymond   31, 74, 85, 99,
101, 103, 120, 129, 130, 131,
157, 158
Brueggemann, Walter   40, 82,
88
Brunner, Emil   23, 63
Buber, Martin   22, 23

Durwell, F. X.   154

Eliot, T.S.   44

Fitzmyer, Joseph   71

Hammarskjöld, Dag   53
Hanson, Paul   139

Minear, Paul   141
Moltmann, Jürgen 59, 60, 156
Murray, John Courtney   78, 79

Noth, Martin   78
Nouwen, Henri 142

Ramsey, A. Michael 89, 164
Richardson, Herbert 15

Taylor, Vincent   156
Thérèse, Sainte   34

von Rad, Gerhard 59